STECK-VAUGHN

SO-BHS-950

Building Strategies
for GED Success

Language Arts, Writing

Steck Vaughn™

A Harcourt Achieve Imprint

www.Steck-Vaughn.com
1-800-531-5015

STAFF CREDITS

Design: Amy Braden, Deborah Diver, Joyce Spicer
Editorial: Gabrielle Field, Heera Kang, Ellen Northcutt

PHOTOGRAPHY

Page 11 ©Jim West/Alamy Images; p.29 ©Ariel Skelley/CORBIS; p.38 ©Jim West/Alamy Images; p.47 ©Emmanuel Faure/Getty Images; p.61 ©Benelux Press/IndexStock; p.84r ©Topham/The Image Works; p.84l ©Ted Spiegel/CORBIS; p.84m ©Francis Benjamin Johnson/CORBIS; p.86m ©Allan Schien/CORBIS; p.86b ©Frank Whitney/Getty Images; p.89 ©Bettmann/CORBIS; p.98 ©John Gress/CORBIS; p.115 ©Robert Barclay/Grant Heilman Photography; p.124 ©Getty Images; p.126 ©Robert Barclay/Grant Heilman Photography.

Additional photography by Royalty Free/Getty Images; Royalty Free/Index Stock.

ILLUSTRATION

All art created by Element, LLC.

ISBN 1-4190-0797-1

Building Strategies is a registered trademark of Harcourt Achieve.

Contents

To the Learner

Congratulations! You have taken an important step as a lifelong learner. You have made the important decision to improve your writing skills. Read below to find out how Steck-Vaughn *Building Strategies for GED Success: Language Arts, Writing* will help you do just that.

- Take the **Pretest** on pages 3–9. Find out which skills you already know and which ones you need to practice. Mark them on the **Skills Preview Chart** on page 10.

- Study the four units in the book. Learn about the parts of a sentence, complete sentences, capitalization, punctuation, spelling, and writing paragraphs. Check out the **GED Tips**—they've got lots of helpful information.

- Complete the **GED Skill Strategy** and **GED Test-Taking Strategy** sections. You'll learn important reading, thinking, and test-taking skills.

- As you work through the book, use the **Answers and Explanations** at the back of the book to check your own work. Study the explanations to have a better understanding of the concepts. You can also use the **Glossary** on page 147 when you want to check the meaning of a word.

- Review what you've learned by taking the **Posttest** on pages 140–145. Use the **Skills Review Chart** on page 146 to see the progress you've made!

Setting Goals

A goal is something that you want to achieve. It's important to set goals in life to help you get what you want. It's also important to set goals for your learning, so think carefully about what your goal is. Setting clear goals is an important part of your success. Choose your goal from those listed below. If you don't see your goal, write it on the line. You may have more than one goal.

My writing goal is to

- get my GED
- improve my personal writing skills
- improve my writing skills at my job

_____

A goal can take a long time to complete. To make achieving your goal easier, you can break your goal into small steps. By focusing on one step at a time, you are able to move closer and closer to achieving your goal.

Steps to your goal can include

- understanding basic grammar rules
- improving your spelling
- improving your punctuation
- learning to write good paragraphs
- helping your children with their writing

We hope that what you learn in this book will help you reach all of your goals.

Now take the *Writing Pretest* on pages 3–9. This will help you know what skills you need to improve so that you can reach your goals.

Writing Pretest

This *Writing Pretest* will give you an idea of the kind of work you will be doing in this book. It will show you your writing strengths. It will also show you which writing skills you need to improve.

The *Writing Pretest* is divided into sections that check what you already know about different writing skills. Each of these sections has a short description and some tips for answering the questions. The pretest also asks you to write a paragraph.

Before you begin each section of the pretest, read the description and the tips to help you focus on the skills being tested. Then read the directions. Read each question carefully before answering it. There is no time limit.

Part A: Nouns, Pronouns, and Adjectives

Nouns are words that identify people, places, things, and ideas. Nouns can be singular or plural. Some nouns change spelling when the plural ending is added or have an irregular plural form.

Pronouns take the place of nouns. A pronoun has a subject form, an object form, and a possessive form. The form depends on the way the pronoun is used in the sentence.

Adjectives are words that describe nouns or pronouns. Adjectives tell *which one, what kind,* or *how many*.

Look for plural nouns that are spelled incorrectly.

Each sentence below has one spelling error. Circle the errors.

1. I carried the boxs upstairs.
2. Ladys and gentlemen, please sit down.
3. Cut the sandwich into two halfs.
4. My childs are old enough to go to school.

Put pronouns in the correct form for the sentence.

Underline the word that correctly completes each sentence.

5. She and (he / him) met last year.
6. Can you go shopping with Anna and (I / me)?
7. (She / Her) apartment is nearby.
8. (We / Us) work in the same building.

Look for words that describe nouns.

Underline the adjectives in each sentence.

9. They live in a big red brick house.
10. This long wool scarf is mine.
11. My new shoes are comfortable.

Part B: Verbs and Adverbs

The verb tells what the sentence's subject (the person or thing that the sentence is about) is doing. Verbs have different forms and different tenses, for example, *call* (present tense), *called* (past tense), *will call* (future tense).

The form of the verb must agree with, or match, the subject. For example, *he calls* is correct. *He call* is not.

Adverbs describe verbs, usually by telling *how*. Adverbs often end in *-ly*. *Slowly* and *carefully* are adverbs.

Each sentence below uses a verb or an adverb incorrectly. Circle the errors.

12. Walter try to call you last night.

13. She worked at her day job next week.

14. They working late every day.

15. Nate and Vera is married.

16. Neither Nate's parents nor Vera's mother live nearby.

17. My children, but not my wife, has red hair.

18. Rosa speaks soft.

19. Kim changed the tire quick.

20. Sudden, he jumped up.

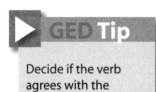

GED Tip

Decide if the verb agrees with the subject.

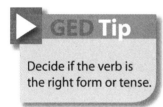

GED Tip

Decide if the verb is the right form or tense.

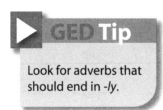

GED Tip

Look for adverbs that should end in *-ly*.

Part C: Complete Sentences

Complete sentences have a subject and a predicate and express a complete thought. The verb in the predicate agrees with the subject.

Not all groups of words are sentences. Sentence fragments are missing either a subject or a predicate or do not express a complete thought. Run-on sentences have a subject, a predicate, and express a complete thought, but they contain two or more complete sentences without the proper punctuation.

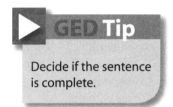

Decide if the sentence is complete.

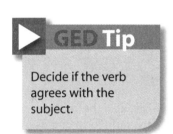

Decide if the verb agrees with the subject.

Look for sentence fragments.

Look for run-on sentences.

Write C if the sentence is correct. Write I if the sentence is incorrect.

_____ **21.** He went home.

_____ **22.** Applied for a job.

_____ **23.** We stayed at home we watched television.

_____ **24.** I washed the car and I waxed it.

_____ **25.** Tigers are cats they have stripes.

Underline the word that correctly completes each sentence.

26. The movie (start / starts) in ten minutes.

27. I (am / is) not working this weekend.

28. She (watch / watches) the news on TV.

29. They can (walk / walks) to work.

30. We (has / have) two children.

Part D: Capitalization and Punctuation

Capitalize the first word in a sentence. Also capitalize words that name a specific person (*Janice*), place (*Miami*), or date (*May 2*).

Punctuation is used in sentences to make the writing easier to read. Punctuation marks include commas, periods, question marks, exclamation points, apostrophes, and quotation marks.

Each sentence has one error. Circle the errors.

31. the bus stop is across Main Street.
32. My birthday is in july.
33. My Husband drives a bus.
34. I made an appointment with dr. Shih.
35. When is thanksgiving?
36. Do I turn right or left at the corner.
37. I borrowed Marys radio.
38. We bought bread, ham, and cheese, at the store.
39. "I got a new job, said Manny."
40. It is time to stop, and clean up.

GED Tip

Look for words that are capitalized. Be sure they begin a sentence or name something specific.

GED Tip

Correct punctuation marks that are used incorrectly. Also correct sentences that are missing a punctuation mark.

Part E: Spelling

Using spelling rules can help you to spell some words. Pronouncing words correctly also helps you include all the syllables when you spell a word. You may need to memorize the spelling of other words.

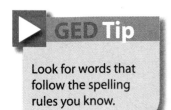

GED Tip

Look for words that follow the spelling rules you know.

Each sentence below has one spelling error. Circle the misspelled words.

41. Please develope this film.

42. The recipe says to seperate the eggs.

43. That man looks familier.

44. Did you recieve a package from the warehouse?

45. Her grandmother's ring is valuble.

46. I am realy too tired to go with you.

47. She preferrs chicken to fish.

48. Aldo is fourty years old.

49. He is allready a citizen.

50. The calandar on the wall has nice pictures.

GED Tip

Pronounce words to see if syllables have been left out.

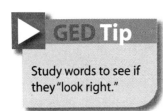

GED Tip

Study words to see if they "look right."

Part F: Writing Paragraphs

51. Write a paragraph about a job you have or would like to have. Begin with a topic sentence that tells what the job is, for example, "I am a nurse's aide" or "I would like to run a car-repair shop." Then write four or five other sentences telling why you like the work and why you are good at it.

_____

_____

_____

_____

_____

_____

_____

_____

_____

_____

_____

_____

_____

_____

_____

_____

_____

_____

_____

When you finish the _Writing Pretest_, check your answers on page 149. Then look at the chart on page 10.

Skills Preview Chart

This chart shows you which writing skills you need to study. Check your answers. In the first column, circle the number of any questions you missed. Then look across the row to find out which skills you should review as well as the page numbers on which you can find instruction on those skills.

Questions	Skill	Pages
1, 2, 3, 4, 5, 6, 7, 8, 9, 10, 11	Nouns, Pronouns, and Adjectives	14–31
12, 13, 14, 15, 16, 17, 18, 19, 20	Verbs and Adverbs	32–49
21, 22, 23, 24, 25, 26, 27, 28, 29, 30	Complete Sentences	12–13, 58–69
31, 32, 33, 34, 35	Capitalization	78–89
36, 37, 38, 39, 40	Punctuation	90–99, 108–109
41, 42, 43, 44, 45, 46, 47, 48, 49, 50	Spelling	100–107
51	Writing Paragraphs	116–131

Unit 1

Grammar and Usage

noun

adverb

subject

plural

Sentences are made up of different types of words. Nouns are words that name people, places, things, and ideas. Adjectives describe nouns. *Happy, soft, cold,* and *tired* are adjectives.

List some adjectives that describe you.

_____

_____

Verbs tell the action of the sentence. *Run, laugh, teach,* and *do* are verbs. Adverbs such as *quickly* and *softly* describe verbs.

Write verbs with adverbs that tell what you like to do. For instance, you may like to *jog slowly* or to *sing loudly.*

_____

_____

sentence
a group of words that contains a subject, a verb, and a complete thought

subject
the person or thing that a sentence is about

predicate
the words that tell what the subject is or does. The predicate includes the verb

noun
a word that names a person, place, thing, or idea

verb
the word that shows action or a state of being

A **sentence** is the basic building block of good writing. To be a complete sentence, a group of words must tell a complete thought.

Example: Not a Complete Thought
■ Making pasta.

Example: Complete Thought
■ Tony is making pasta.

Complete sentences are made up of a **subject**, a **predicate**, and a complete thought.

The subject of a sentence is the person or thing that the sentence is about. The subject is a **noun**. The subject of the sentence below is underlined.

Example: <u>Tim</u> is the oldest of three children.

Underline the subject in each sentence below.

1. Greg plays the piano.

2. Bicycles are popular in my city.

The predicate tells what the subject is or is doing. The predicate contains the **verb**. The predicate in the sentence below is underlined. The verb is circled.

Example: The neighbor (knocked) <u>on the door.</u>

Underline the predicate in each sentence below. Then circle the verb.

3. Jerome plays guitar in a jazz band.

4. The band is very talented.

5. Ali smiled at her friend.

Are the following complete sentences? Write *yes* or *no*.

6. The newspaper is on the table. _____

7. The article says our taxes will rise. _____

8. Thinks about a move to the South. _____

Check your answers on page 150.

Underline the subject in each sentence.

1. She is very clumsy.

2. Alec doesn't like horror movies.

3. Fruit is always part of my breakfast.

4. You need to take this home.

5. Nora wants to be a doctor someday.

Underline the predicate in each sentence. Then circle the verb.

6. Joan is Steven's friend.

7. Steven teaches kindergarten.

8. He drives his car to work.

9. The car broke down yesterday.

10. Joan took him to work.

Write a complete sentence that answers the question. Be sure to use a subject, a predicate, and a complete thought.

11. Where would you like to live someday?

_____

_____

12. What do you like about your home?

_____

_____

13. Who is one person that you really admire?

_____

_____

GED Tip

Many questions on the GED Writing Test require you to identify the subject and the predicate in a sentence. Practice this skill.

Check your answers on page 150.

Read the following sentences.

- Anita wrote.
- Wilbur ate.

Although the sentences are short, they are complete sentences. They each have a subject and a predicate. However, the sentences don't tell you much. Read the sentences again and think of something you could add to each one.

Anita wrote _____ .

Wilbur ate _____ .

Here are ways you might have added to the sentences.

Anita wrote a letter.
Wilbur ate a sandwich.

object
a word that receives the action of the verb in a sentence

The words that you added to each sentence are the **objects** of the sentences. The object of a sentence tells who or what receives the action of the verb. Think of the object of the sentence as the thing that has something done to it. Adding objects to sentences gives the reader a more complete picture of what is happening. When you add an object to a sentence, you add it to the predicate. The predicate includes the verb and the object.

The subjects, verbs, and objects for the sentences above are shown below.

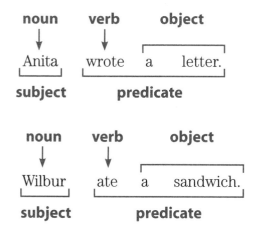

Nouns can be subjects or objects in sentences. The subjects of the sentences below are underlined. **Circle the objects.**

1. <u>Doris</u> read the memo.

2. <u>Three people</u> attended the meeting.

3. <u>Bob</u> wrote a report.

The nouns you circled can be subjects in other sentences. **Read these examples. Underline the subjects.**

4. The memo was four pages long.

5. The meeting lasted a long time.

6. Bob's report is a good one.

Use each of the following nouns to write two sentences. In the first sentence, use the noun as the subject of the sentence. In the second sentence, use the noun as the object.

7. telephone

   _____

   _____

8. water

   _____

   _____

9. chair

   _____

   _____

10. Kate

   _____

   _____

Check your answers on page 150.

compound subject
two or more subjects, usually joined by *and* or *or*

compound object
two or more objects, usually joined by *and* or *or*

Some sentences have two or more subjects or objects. These are called **compound subjects** or **compound objects**.

Examples:

- Compound subject: <u>Tom and Bea</u> went home.
- Compound object: Do you remember <u>Ed, Sue, and Jack</u>?

Write a sentence about people you know. Use a compound subject.

_____

_____

Write a sentence about events you remember. Use a compound object.

_____

_____

You know that nouns identify people, places, things, and ideas. There are two kinds of nouns—common nouns and proper nouns. Common nouns give general names. Proper nouns give specific names.

Common Nouns	Proper Nouns
actor	Tom Hanks
city	Chicago
month	November

Notice that the proper nouns begin with capital letters.

Write proper nouns for these common nouns.

1. musician _____

2. street _____

3. friend _____

4. restaurant _____

Check your answers on page 150.

When you write about more than one person, place, thing, or idea, you use a **plural** noun. You usually add -*s* to a **singular** noun to make it plural.

Examples:

■ mops   gorillas   rivers   boys

Write the plural forms.

1. apple _____   2. truck _____

3. day _____   4. hat _____

If a noun ends in *s*, *sh*, *ch*, or *x*, you add -*es* to form the plural.

Examples:

■ buses   wishes   beaches   boxes

Write the plural forms.

5. dish _____   6. inch _____

7. tax _____   8. miss _____

For nouns that end in *y* and have a **consonant** before the *y*, drop the *y* and add -*ies*.

Examples:

■ activity ⟶ activities   ■ party ⟶ parties

Write the plural forms.

9. city _____   10. fly_____

11. baby _____   12. lily _____

Check your answers on page 150.

plural
more than one

singular
only one

vowel
one of these letters of the alphabet: *a, e, i, o, u*

consonant
any letter of the alphabet that isn't a vowel

For words that end in *f* or *fe*, drop the *f* or *fe* and add *-ves*.

Examples:

■ life ⟶ li**ves**

■ loaf ⟶ loa**ves**

Write the plurals.

1. wife _____

2. calf _____

3. wolf _____

4. shelf _____

Not all nouns follow these rules for forming plurals. These nouns are **exceptions**. Below are some common irregular plurals. Note that some nouns have the same singular and plural forms.

exception
something that doesn't follow a rule

Some Irregular Plurals	
Singular	**Plural**
roof	roofs
belief	beliefs
woman	women
man	men
child	children
foot	feet
tooth	teeth
goose	geese
mouse	mice
deer	deer
fish	fish
sheep	sheep

▶ **GED Tip**

Practice using plurals in your writing so that you use them correctly on the GED Writing Test.

Write the plurals.

5. foot _____

6. woman _____

7. belief _____

8. deer _____

Check your answers on page 150.

Practice

Underline the subject. Then circle the object.

1. Danita borrows books from the library every week.

2. The librarian sorts new novels.

3. Her children like the trips to the library.

4. They read books about animals and sports.

5. The library has magazines too.

6. Many people borrow CDs.

7. Mr. Garcia borrows DVDs.

8. Libraries inspire people to learn.

Write proper nouns for the following common nouns.

9. city_____

10. singer_____

**Write a sentence about places you know or have visited.
Use a compound subject.**

11. _____

_____

**Write a sentence about something you and your friends have done.
Use a compound object.**

12. _____

_____

Write the correct plural for each noun.

13. friend _____ 14. watch _____

15. man _____ 16. factory_____

17. key _____ 18. life _____

Check your answers on page 150.

possession
ownership or belonging

apostrophe
a punctuation mark that can be used to show possession or ownership

You can make a noun show ownership, or **possession**, by using an **apostrophe (')**.

Add an apostrophe and an s ('s) to the end of a singular noun to form the possessive.

Example:

■ the book that Jan owns ⟶ <u>Jan's</u> book

Write the possessive form of each noun.

1. woman ⟶ _____

2. worker ⟶ _____

3. car ⟶ _____

4. Dr. White ⟶ _____

Add 's to the end of a singular noun if the noun ends in s.

Example:

■ the watch that Thomas owns ⟶ <u>Thomas's</u> watch

Write the possessive form of each noun.

5. bus _____

6. radiator _____

7. Silas _____

8. Uncle Chris _____

9. bird _____

10. Mrs. Jones _____

11. brother _____

12. shop _____

Check your answers on page 151.

Plural nouns can also show possession. To form the possessive of a plural noun ending in *s,* add an apostrophe to the end of the word.

Examples:

- homes of the families ⟶ <u>families'</u> homes
- habitat of the wolves ⟶ <u>wolves'</u> habitat

Write the possessive form of each noun.

1. benches ⟶ _____

2. cities ⟶ _____

3. Johnsons ⟶ _____

Complete each sentence with the possessive form of the noun.

4. Listen to those _____ meows. (cats)

5. Please trim the _____ apple tree. (Smiths)

6. Mary folded both _____ laundry. (girls)

Be careful not to confuse a possessive with a plural. Although a plural noun and a possessive noun might sound the same when heard out loud or in your head, remember that they have different meanings.

Example: Incorrectly Used Possessive

All of the <u>boy's</u> have arrived at the party.
(There is no possession or ownership in this sentence.)

Example: Correctly Used Plural

All of the <u>boys</u> have arrived at the party.
(The plural shows that more than one boy arrived.)

GED Tip

Don't confuse plurals and possessives on the GED Writing Test. Make sure that an apostrophe is used to show possession.

Choose the correct noun to complete each sentence.

7. Most of the (dog's / dogs) food was eaten.

8. Both (player's / players) tried hard to win.

Check your answers on page 151.

Some plural nouns do not end in *s*. To form the possessives of these nouns, add an apostrophe and an *s*.

Examples:

- children → <u>children's</u> shoe
- men → <u>men's</u> shoes

Write the possessive form of the noun.

1. women _____

2. mice _____

3. deer _____

4. feet _____

5. Lucas _____

6. cook _____

7. beaches _____

8. grandchildren _____

9. moose _____

Complete each sentence with the possessive form of the noun.

10. This fall we must shear the _____ wool. (sheep)

11. The candidate supports _____ rights. (people)

12. Light the match with the _____ tip. (match)

13. Exercise has improved their _____ health. (wives)

14. Ana coaches the _____ track team. (girls)

Check your answers on page 151.

Practice

Underline the noun that correctly completes each sentence.

1. Last week was our (companies / company's) picnic.

2. All of the (activity's / activities) were fun.

3. Mr. Wall welcomed the (employees' / employee's) families.

4. Sondra Jones ran the (childrens' / children's) games.

5. The children loved Ms. (Jones' / Jones's) idea.

6. We watched the (women's / womens') skit while we ate.

7. Everyone crowded to hear the (boss's / boss') speech.

8. Mr. (Walls / Wall's) speech inspired us all.

Write the possessive form of each noun.

9. groups _____

10. men _____

11. Isabel _____

12. mother _____

13. calves _____

Complete each sentence with the possessive form of the noun.

14. Many of our _____ parks are in poor shape. (city)

15. _____ Field, for instance, is full of ruts and holes. (Mill)

16. With _____ help, we can improve the parks. (people)

17. Citizens will gather next week to discuss _____ ideas. (everyone)

18. We will also discuss Mayor _____ plan for the parks. (Andreas)

19. The group will choose the _____ best features. (plan)

20. The _____ plan puts safety first. (mayor)

21. A _____ safety is very important. (child)

Check your answers on page 151.

pronoun
a word that can replace a noun in a sentence

personal pronoun
a pronoun that replaces either the subject noun or the object noun in a sentence

subject pronoun
a pronoun that replaces the subject in a sentence

object pronoun
a pronoun that replaces the object in a sentence

A **pronoun** is a word that takes the place of a noun. Below is a chart of **personal pronouns**. A **subject pronoun** takes the place of the subject of a sentence. An **object pronoun** takes the place of an object.

Subject Pronouns	Object Pronouns
I	me
you	you
he, she, it	him, her, it
we	us
you	you
they	them

Read the following sentences. Pay close attention to how the pronouns replace the nouns.

Greg took the children to the library.
He took them to the library.

Replace the underlined noun with the correct pronoun.

1. The drivers approached their racing cars. _____

2. Emilio got into his car and started the car. _____

3. Bette doesn't like the beach. _____

Read the paragraph. Underline the subject pronouns. Then circle the object pronouns.

Anna and I had a picnic in the park. We laid the blanket down. Unfortunately, we laid it on an ant bed. The ants weren't too happy with us. They crawled all over the blanket. Anna was supposed to bring popsicles, but she forgot them at home. Anna and I decided that next time, we would let someone else plan the picnic.

Check your answers on page 151.

Here is a chart of **possessive pronouns**. A possessive pronoun takes the place of a noun that shows ownership or possession.

Possessive Pronouns	
my, mine	our, ours
your, yours	your, yours
his, her, hers, its	their, theirs

A possessive pronoun can take the place of a noun that is the subject of a sentence.

Example:

- Jim and Amy's car is blue. → Their car is blue.

A possessive pronoun can also take the place of a noun that is the object of a sentence.

Example:

- The blue car is Jim and Amy's. → The blue car is theirs.

Change the underlined words to possessive pronouns.

1. Mrs. Bell's husband is not home. _____

2. Monica and Pat's anniversary is today. _____

3. This house is Ben and Carrie's. _____

4. I found a dog's collar. _____

5. Alan's glasses didn't break. _____

The noun that a pronoun replaces is the **antecedent**.

Examples:

- Grace and Eli are coworkers. They work at the library.
  (*Grace and Eli* is the antecedent of *they.*)
- The van belongs to Peter and Cy. It is theirs.
  (*Van* is the antecedent of *it; Peter and Cy* is the antecedent of *theirs.*)

Check your answers on page 151.

A pronoun needs to match its antecedent. For example, if the noun is plural, the antecedent should be plural. When a pronoun matches its antecedent, the noun and pronoun are said to have **noun–pronoun agreement**.

noun–pronoun agreement
a noun and a pronoun that have the same number and gender (male or female or neutral)

Example: Incorrect Agreement

The Boy Scout earned their merit badge.

Since *Boy Scout* is a singular noun, a singular pronoun should be used.

Example: Correct Agreement

The Boy Scout earned his merit badge.

Underline the correct pronoun. Then circle its antecedent.

1. Tyrone and I decided to replace (her / our) dishwasher.

2. The dishwasher was old, and (they / it) leaked water onto the floor.

3. My neighbor said (she / we / us) found a good dishwasher at B&B Appliances.

4. The salespeople there know what (he / they / I) are doing.

5. After Tyrone and I purchased the dishwasher, (we / they / he) went next door.

6. The shop next door was new, and (they / she / it) had many interesting things.

7. The owner of the shop said (we / our / she) used to travel all over the world.

8. She had rugs from India, and (they / us / it) were beautiful.

9. I wanted to buy a purple rug, but (I / he / you) didn't see any.

10. Tyrone bought a decorated pot for (his / yours / their) garden.

Check your answers on page 152.

GED Tip

Remember that the pronoun *they* must refer to a plural noun. Do not use *they* to refer to a singular noun.

Practice

Underline the correct pronoun to complete each sentence.

1. You and (I / me) should make plans.

2. (We / Us) have to shop for groceries.

3. The doctor wants to speak with you and (I / me).

4. We want to go with (they / them).

5. Mine is ready. (Your / Yours) will be ready soon.

6. (He / Him) told (she / her) to come to the meeting.

Underline the correct pronoun. Then circle its antecedent.

7. This work is hard because (they / it) requires both brains and muscles.

8. The bosses ask a lot from (their / her) employees.

9. When Arturo and John asked for time off, (he / they) were denied.

10. Each man must be able to do (his / their) own measurements and calculations.

Underline the pronoun. Then circle its antecedent.

11. The doctor answered her phone.

12. When Oscar left, he took the car.

13. Lily and Sam hated their costumes.

Write the correct possessive pronoun for the underlined noun.

14. The cat's scratching post belongs in the bedroom. _____

15. Vera didn't want to lose Vera's keys. _____

16. The children played with the children's toys. _____

17. Paul's book is on the table. _____

18. Gina's and my favorite show is on. _____

Check your answers on page 152.

adjective
a word that describes a noun or pronoun by telling *which one, what kind,* or *how many*

An **adjective** is a word that describes a noun or pronoun. An adjective gives more detail about the noun or pronoun it describes.

Example: The <u>nervous</u>, <u>young</u> actress got the part.

(*Nervous* and *young* describe the noun *actress.*)

An adjective can also come after the word it describes.

Example: The book is <u>thick</u> and <u>heavy</u>.

(*Thick* and *heavy* describe the noun *book.*)

Adjectives add interest to your sentences and help the reader picture what you are describing. For example, look at all the adjectives on the menu for Kathy's Café.

Kathy's Café

Monday Special

Juicy grilled hamburger
on fresh multi-grain bun

Crisp hot French fries

Tossed green salad

Iced Tea

$8.95

Cross out the adjectives in Monday's menu.

With the adjectives crossed out, the menu just lists *hamburger, bun, fries, salad, coffee,* and *tea.* By themselves, these words do not sound as tasty.

Imagine you work at Kathy's Café. **Write your own adjectives to describe the dishes in Tuesday's special.**

_____ fish

_____ potatoes

_____ beans

_____ salad

_____ coffee

_____ ice cream

Check your answers on page 152.

Adjectives add detail that describes how someone or something looks, sounds, smells, tastes, or feels.

Add adjectives to these sentences. The first one is done for you.

1. Thanksgiving dinner was <u>delicious</u> and <u>hectic</u>.

2. Mom's clean house smelled _____.

3. The turkey was _____ and _____.

4. My _____ nephews were _____.

5. Mom's _____ dog barked loudly.

6. For dessert I had _____ apple pie.

7. At the end of the night, I felt _____.

The words *this, that, these,* and *those* are also adjectives. They must agree, or make sense, with the nouns they describe. *This* and *that* agree with singular nouns.

Examples:

■ this house
■ that girl

When writing about two or more things, use *these* or *those*.

Examples:

■ these houses
■ those girls

Underline the word that correctly completes each sentence.

8. We have worked on (this / those) car a long time.

9. Look at (this / these) flat tires.

10. (That / Those) fenders are dented too.

11. (This / These) cars are very hard to find.

12. We want (this / these) car to be perfect.

Check your answers on page 152.

Place the adjective near the word it describes, or the sentence may be confusing. In the examples below, what word is described by *expensive* and *fast*?

Example: Confusing Placement

The car, says Ray, who is a mechanic, is <u>expensive</u> and <u>fast</u>.

Example: Correct Placement

The car is <u>expensive</u> and <u>fast</u>, says Ray, who is a mechanic.

Rewrite each sentence so that the underlined adjectives are close to the words they describe.

1. One job at Pro Line that is <u>important</u> is sorting the mail.

    _____

    _____

2. The job on your list is to sort the mail <u>first</u>.

    _____

    _____

3. This mail must be delivered now that is <u>important</u>.

    _____

    _____

4. All boxes must be recycled that are <u>cardboard</u>.

    _____

    _____

Write a sentence for each of the adjectives.

5. happy

    _____

6. second

    _____

7. little

    _____

► **GED Tip**

Use adjectives when you write on the GED Writing Test. Adjectives make your writing interesting. They also help the reader picture what you are writing about.

Check your answers on page 152.

Underline the word that correctly completes each sentence.

1. Bring the patient (these / that) tray of food.

2. We expect him to run for mayor (this / those) year.

3. (This / These) cars are very popular.

4. (This / Those) mountains are high.

5. I will wear (this / these) shirt and (that / those) tie.

Add an adjective to complete each sentence.

6. That man is _____ .

7. Her coat looks _____ .

8. My new pet is a _____ cat.

9. The weather is very _____ .

10. We went to see the _____ movie.

11. The _____ party lasted very late.

12. The firefighters were _____ .

Underline the adjectives in each sentence.

13. Stacey has a small, tidy desk.

14. The new neighbors seem nice.

15. Those little boys are brothers.

16. They have brown hair and blue eyes.

17. Puerto Rico has many beautiful, sandy beaches.

18. It also contains a tropical rain forest.

19. In the rain forest are rare birds and big, colorful flowers.

20. The paper advertised for a hardworking, experienced printer.

Check your answers on page 153.

Most verbs have four forms. The four forms of the verb *call* are in the chart below.

Verb (base form)	Present Participle	Past	Past Participle
call	calling	called	called

base form
the simple form of the verb without any endings

Use the **base form** of a verb when you are writing about *I, you, we,* or *they* in the **present tense**.

Examples:
- I <u>call</u> her every day.
- They <u>call</u> less frequently.

tense
the form of the verb that shows the time of its action

Add *-s* to the base form of the verb when you are writing a sentence with *he, she,* or *it* as the subject.

present tense
the forms of a verb that expresses present time

Examples:
- He call<u>s</u> often.
- She feel<u>s</u> better.
- It still hurt<u>s</u>.

future tense
the forms of a verb that expresses future time

Also use the base form for *I, you, he, she, it, we,* and *they* in the **future tense**.

Examples:
- I <u>will call</u> next week.
- He <u>should call</u> tomorrow.
- They <u>will call</u> later today.

Use the base form for a command.

Example:
- <u>Call</u> when you arrive.

The present participle is the form of the verb ending in *-ing*. Use the present participle to show that an action is continuing. Use it with any subject.

Examples:
- We'll be ca<u>lling</u> you.
- I'm ca<u>lling</u> her now.
- You are wor<u>king</u>.

The **past tense** of a verb often has the same form as the past-participle of a verb. Often, they both end in *-ed*. The past participle is used with the **helping verb** *have*.

Examples:
- He <u>called</u> yesterday. (past)
- I <u>have called</u> you several times. (past participle)
- <u>Has</u> she <u>called</u> you? (past participle)

past tense
the forms of a verb that express past time

helping verb
a verb like *have*, *be*, and *do* that is used with other verbs

regular verb
a verb that has the *-ed* ending in the past tense and past participle

Underline the verb in each sentence. Then write the base form of each verb.

1. Tom <u>seems</u> happy._____seem_____
2. Sandy passed the mall on her way home. _____
3. She has painted only one wall so far. _____
4. Are they looking for an apartment? _____
5. No, they are waiting until summer. _____
6. They are saving their money first. _____
7. Jane and Alexander clapped their hands in joy. _____
8. Kelly is listening to her music. _____
9. He has decided not to go. _____
10. Are you talking to us? _____

The verbs in the exercise above are all **regular verbs**. The past forms of regular verbs always end in *-ed*.

Check your answers on page 153.

irregular verb
a verb that doesn't have the -ed ending in the past tense and past participle

The past forms of **irregular verbs** do not end in -ed. Each irregular verb has its own past-tense form. The chart of irregular verbs below shows the different forms for each verb.

Some Irregular Verbs					
Base Form	**Past Tense**	**Past Participle**	**Base Form**	**Past Tense**	**Past Participle**
be	was, were	been	lie	lay	lain
become	became	become	make	made	made
begin	began	begun	meet	met	met
catch	caught	caught	put	put	put
come	came	come	rise	rose	risen
do	did	done	see	saw	seen
drive	drove	driven	send	sent	sent
eat	ate	eaten	sit	sat	sat
feel	felt	felt	take	took	taken
get	got	got/gotten	tell	told	told
go	went	gone	think	thought	thought
have	had	had	understand	understood	understood
know	knew	known	win	won	won
lay	laid	laid	write	wrote	written

Underline the verb in each sentence. Then write the base form of each verb. Use the chart above to help you.

11. He <u>drove</u> to work. _____drive_____

12. It began to rain. _____

13. He has written the report. _____

14. We won by two points! _____

15. I sent the letter by airmail. _____

16. They met at the bowling alley. _____

17. The sweater felt soft. _____

18. Aaron thinks highly of you. _____

19. They have become best friends. _____

20. Alice and Kim had a great time. _____

Check your answers on page 153.

The past participle is used with a helping verb (see page 33). The past-participle forms can be difficult to remember. Use the chart on page 34 to help you.

▶ GED **Tip**

Learn as many irregular verbs forms as you can. Knowing these forms will help when you take the GED Writing Test.

Complete the following sentences. Use the past participle of the verb.

1. He has ___gone___ home. (go)

2. We have just _____ to eat. (begin)

3. I haven't _____ him for long. (know)

4. She has _____ her dog home. (take)

5. I hope you haven't _____ my cold. (catch)

Verbs tell *what* is happening. Their forms tell *when* it is happening.

Examples:
- We <u>arrived</u> late. (past)
- We usually <u>arrive</u> on time. (present)
- We <u>will arrive</u> early tomorrow. (future)

Identify the tense of each sentence. Write *past, present,* or *future*.

6. I checked our supplies. _____

7. There was only one box of pencils left. _____

8. I check stock every month. _____

9. It is my job to make sure we don't run out. _____

10. I will order more pencils. _____

11. I called you last night. _____

12. I will mail the birthday card tomorrow. _____

Check your answers on page 154.

Write the base forms of the verbs in these sports headlines.

1. Rivera Hits Two Home Runs   _____

2. Tracy Prepares for Next Match   _____

3. Duke Defeats Kansas   _____

4. Lang Injures Back   _____

5. Whalers Lose to Capitals   _____

6. *Giants Win!*   _____

7. Davis Has Knee Surgery   _____

8. *Cardinals Sweep Series*   _____

Underline the form of the verb that correctly completes each sentence.

9. On our way to work, it (begin / began / begun) to rain.

10. We will (see / saw / seen) you next week.

11. I (sleep / slept) late yesterday.

12. Did you (find / found) your gloves?

13. You said you had (lose / lost) them.

14. I (get / got) a letter from my uncle yesterday.

15. He (fall / fell / fallen) on some ice.

16. He (strike / struck) his elbow on the sidewalk.

17. Fortunately, his elbow wasn't (break / broke / broken).

18. Marie (say / said) she would be working late today.

19. Has anyone (come / came) to pick up the mail?

20. My mother (teach / taught) me to work hard.

Check your answers on page 154.

Write the correct form of the verb in parentheses.

21. Last month, my supervisor _____ me
    into her office. (call)

22. She _____ to talk with me about
    something. (want)

23. Of course, I _____ a little nervous. (be)

24. She said, "Next month, you _____ a
    new job title." (have)

25. The manager has _____ an assistant
    since January. (need)

26. My supervisor _____ me for this
    promotion. (recommend)

27. Someday I know I _____ a manager. (be)

Rewrite the paragraph in the past tense.

   Maria and David watch a television program on Channel 5.
The show is about race car drivers. The show's host speaks with
several well–known drivers. The stories of these men and women are
fascinating. Maria says she hopes to race cars professionally some day.
David is more interested in fixing and maintaining race cars. David and
Maria talk for hours about their plans for their future in car racing.

_____

_____

_____

_____

_____

_____

_____

Check your answers on page 154.

Sometimes the verbs *be* and *have* "help" other verbs. Look at the following examples.

- I <u>am</u> <u>hurrying</u>.
- We <u>have</u> <u>reviewed</u> your letter.

You can use helping verbs in the past, present, or future tenses. The chart below shows how to use the regular verb *work* in each tense. The helping verbs *be* and *have* are underlined.

Past Tense	Present Tense	Future Tense
I <u>was</u> working.	I <u>am</u> working.	I <u>will</u> <u>be</u> working.
I <u>had</u> worked.	I <u>have</u> worked.	I <u>will</u> <u>have</u> worked.
You <u>were</u> working.	You <u>are</u> working.	You <u>will</u> <u>be</u> working.
You <u>had</u> worked.	You <u>have</u> worked.	You <u>will</u> <u>have</u> worked.
He <u>was</u> working.	He <u>is</u> working.	He <u>will</u> <u>be</u> working.
She <u>had</u> worked.	She <u>has</u> worked.	She <u>will</u> <u>have</u> worked.
We <u>were</u> working.	We <u>are</u> working.	We <u>will</u> <u>be</u> working.
They <u>had</u> worked.	They <u>have</u> worked.	They <u>will</u> <u>have</u> worked.

Complete each sentence. Use a form of the verb *work* or *write*.

1. I was _____ at this store when we met.

2. They have _____ him several letters.

3. He has _____ me only once.

4. By Friday you will have _____ for 30 hours this week.

Check your answers on page 154.

Another helping verb is *do* (*did, done*). Sometimes *do* is used to add emphasis. For example, when answering the question *Why didn't you work late last night?*, the statement *I did work late last night* sounds stronger than the statement *I worked late last night.*

Use the helping verb *do* when you write questions and negatives.

Examples:
- <u>Do</u> you <u>have</u> change for a dollar?
- <u>Did</u> you <u>take</u> the car to the garage?
- <u>Doesn't</u> he <u>look</u> like his father?
- I <u>didn't</u> <u>forget</u>.

Be, have, and *do* are the most common helping verbs. Look at this list of other helping verbs.

can	would	shall	may
could	should	must	might

- He <u>should</u> <u>drive</u> more slowly.

These helping verbs also can be used with the helping verbs *be* and *have*.

- He <u>must</u> <u>be</u> <u>driving</u> the children to school.
- He <u>must</u> <u>have</u> <u>driven</u> the children to school.

Circle the verb. Then underline the helping verb or verbs.

1. I may have seen this movie before.
2. Can you help me?
3. Sam might come with us.
4. Would you like some coffee?

Check your answers on page 154.

Change the following sentences from statements to questions.

1. You fixed the leaky faucet.

   Did you fix the leaky faucet?

2. You are copying the reports.

   _____

3. Henry put new tires on the car.

   _____

4. He has been trying to get a new job.

   _____

5. You have met them before.

   _____

6. The judge has arrived in his chambers.

   _____

7. Shelly has told her mother the good news.

   _____

8. They will leave for Miami tomorrow.

   _____

9. I should wake the children now.

   _____

10. They can sleep a little longer.

    _____

Circle the verb. Then underline the helping verb or verbs.

11. Charles <u>may be</u> (joining) the armed services.

12. He has been thinking about it for months.

13. Gerald, his father, might object.

14. He should let Charles decide for himself.

15. Charles's mother must be worrying.

16. She will be turning seventy soon.

Complete each sentence with the correct form of the verb.

17. _____ you take the bus to work yesterday? (Do / Does / Did)

18. _____ they going to deposit the checks? (Am / Is / Are)

19. After today, I _____ worked for one year.
(will be / will have / will)

20. Tomorrow at this time, I _____ on my way to visit Jo.
(will be / will have / have been)

21. Howard _____ painted the whole room by the weekend.
(will / will be / will have)

22. They actually _____ see that movie last night. (do / does / did)

Underline the form of the verb that correctly completes each sentence.

23. I must have (seen / saw) that movie before.

24. They can (help / helped) us.

25. The Russels should (go / going) soon.

26. Have you (been / be) watching your soap opera?

27. That job must (be / being) challenging.

28. Betty would (come / came) if she could.

Write a sentence using the helping verb in parentheses.

29. (would) _____

_____

30. (might) _____

_____

31. (should) _____

_____

32. (must) _____

_____

Check your answers on page 154.

Subject–Verb Agreement

subject-verb agreement
the subject and the verb must agree in number; if the subject is plural, the verb must be in the plural form

Subject-verb agreement is an important part of good writing. Subject-verb agreement means using the correct verb form to match the subject of the sentence. Look at these sentences.

Examples:

- One <u>girl</u> <u>eats</u> alone.
- The <u>girls</u> <u>eat</u> lunch together every day.

Notice that girl eat<u>s</u> and girl<u>s</u> eat. When the subject is singular, the present tense verb ends in *s*. When the subject is plural (more than one), the present tense verb has no *s*.

Choose the correct verb form to complete each sentence.

1. The president _____ a bill into law. (sign / signs)

2. My parents _____ to work every day. (go / goes)

3. My daughter _____ the guitar. (play / plays)

4. My sons _____ hockey. (play / plays)

5. The man _____ every day before work. (run / runs)

6. Children today _____ too much TV. (watch / watches)

7. That person _____ a bus. (drive / drives)

8. Those people _____ on my block. (live / lives)

9. Many women _____ sports. (like / likes)

10. Which student in the class _____ best? (draw / draws)

11. Her son _____ around the house. (help / helps)

12. Our plants _____ the sunshine. (enjoy / enjoys)

Check your answers on page 155.

Subject-verb agreement can be tricky with the present tense of the verbs *be* and *have*. Read the charts below.

Present Tense of the Verb *Be*	
I	am
He She It	is
You We They	are

Present Tense of the Verb *Have*	
I	have
He She It	has
You We They	have

Do not use these incorrect forms: *I be, you be, he be, we be, they be,* and *you is.*

Complete the sentences. Use the correct present–tense form of *be* or *have*.

1. She _____ a senior in high school. (form of *be*)

2. We _____ from Mexico. (form of *be*)

3. I _____ a dentist appointment today.
    (form of *have*)

4. Tom _____ a job as a carpenter. (form of *have*)

5. The women _____ studying. (form of *be*)

The past tense of the verb *have* is always *had*. But the verb *be* has two forms for the past tense: *was* and *were*.

Complete the sentences below using the chart on the right. Use the correct past-tense form of *be*.

6. It _____ snowy yesterday.

7. You _____ not wearing boots.

8. The customers _____ hungry.

9. I _____ a little late.

Check your answers on page 155.

Past Tense of *Be*	
I	was
He She It	was
You We They	were

Most of the time, you add an *-s* to the base form of the verb to make the present tense agree with *he, she, it,* or a singular noun. Sometimes you have to follow the rules for plural nouns.

- Add *-s* to most verbs.
- Add *-es* to verbs that end in *ch* (watch), *sh* (wash), or *s* (pass).
- Drop the *y* and add *-ies* to verbs that end in *y*.

Read the chart below.

Subject	Verb		
	Work	**Watch**	**Worry**
I	work	watch	worry
He She It	works	watches	worries
You We They	work	watch	worry

Some common verbs do not follow these rules: *be, buy, have, can, must, will, may, might,* and *should.*

Complete each sentence with the present-tense form of the verb.

1. She _____ science. (teach)

2. The young man _____ my groceries. (carry)

3. He _____ the baseball. (catch)

4. My girlfriend _____ to work. (walk)

5. He _____ to the train. (hurry)

6. She _____ and dries the dishes. (wash)

Check your answers on page 155.

GED Tip

If you are unsure of the correct verb to use on the GED Writing Test, find the subject and underline it. This will help you to decide which form of the verb agrees with the subject.

Underline the form of the verb that correctly completes each sentence.

1. He (swim / swims) ten laps a day.

2. Trains (arrive / arrives) at Union Station.

3. The movie (start / starts) in ten minutes.

4. Many people (visit / visits) Old Faithful on vacation.

5. I (am / is / be) a secretary.

6. Ms. Ruiz (am / is / be) my boss.

7. They (has / have) two children.

8. The girl (am / is / be) older than the boy.

9. We (was / were) going to tell you about the new movie.

10. (Are / Is) you working this weekend?

11. My TV (has / have) a remote control.

Complete each sentence with the correct form of the verb. Add -s, -es, or -ies.

12. Randy _____ his son at bedtime. (kiss)

13. He _____ for trout in the river. (fish)

14. She _____ her hair. (dry)

15. The customer _____ cough syrup for his cold. (buy)

16. She _____ the movie. (watch)

17. He _____ so he won't be late. (hurry)

18. Dee _____ about getting to work on time. (worry)

Check your answers on page 155.

adverb
a word that describes a verb, an adjective, or another adverb

A word used to describe a verb is an **adverb**. Adverbs describe *how, when, how much,* and *where.* Adverbs often end in *-ly.* For example, *loud* is an adjective, while *loudly* is an adverb. The words *hard, fast,* and *well* are adverbs, too, even though they don't end in *-ly.*

Notice how adverbs add to the meaning of the simple sentence *I work.*

Examples:

- I work <u>quickly</u>.
- I work <u>hard</u> and <u>carefully</u>.

Some special adverbs, such as *very* and *somewhat,* describe other adverbs. Here is a sentence that has six adverbs:

- I <u>usually</u> work <u>hard</u>, <u>very</u> <u>carefully</u>, and <u>somewhat</u> <u>neatly</u>.

Adverbs can also describe adjectives. In the following examples, adverbs are underlined and adjectives are circled.

- You are <u>extremely</u> (clever).
- That house looks <u>very</u> (old).

Add adverbs to these sentences.

1. She always drives _____.

2. He tries to work _____.

3. They spoke _____.

Remember that adjectives describe nouns, while adverbs describe verbs, other adverbs, and adjectives. To change sentences with adjectives to sentences with adverbs, you have to rewrite the sentences.

Examples:

- She is a <u>careful</u> driver. (adjective)
- She drives <u>carefully</u>. (adverb)

Check your answers on page 155.

Underline the adverb to complete each sentence.

1. She thinks (quick/quickly).

2. The paint went on (smooth/smoothly).

3. The television blared (loud/loudly).

4. I (easy/easily) fixed the lamp.

In all four sentences, the first word in the parentheses is an adjective. The second word is an adverb. Only adverbs (*quickly, smoothly, loudly, easily*) can be used to describe verbs. In the above sentences, the adverbs all tell *how* something happened.

Rewrite each sentence with an adverb instead of an adjective.

5. He is a clear speaker.

   _____

6. She is a clever writer.

   _____

Adverbs can be placed almost anywhere in a sentence. If an adverb is the first word in the sentence, put a comma after it. The meaning is the same in all the sentences below. All the sentences are correct.

- Slowly, the man walked down the street.
- The man slowly walked down the street.
- The man walked slowly down the street.

Write the following sentence in three ways. Each time, put the adverb *loudly* in a different place in the sentence.

They laughed at her jokes.

7. _____

8. _____

9. _____

Check your answers on page 155.

Adverbs can make your writing clearer and more interesting. Be sure to include adverbs in your writing when taking the GED Writing Test.

Practice

Change the underlined adjectives to adverbs.

1. <u>Sudden</u>, Willa woke up. _____

2. She got dressed <u>immediate</u>. _____

3. We spoke <u>soft</u> around the sleeping baby. _____

4. He is <u>complete</u> exhausted. _____

5. Hank <u>patient</u> waxed the car. _____

6. Dan works <u>accurate</u>. _____

7. He <u>careful</u> measures the wood. _____

Underline the word that correctly completes each sentence.

8. I (quick / quickly) took the bus to work.

9. Amos cut his hand (badly / bad).

10. He was (real / really) afraid it would get infected.

11. She does her job (careful / carefully).

12. They don't (usually / usual) work on weekends.

13. He (easy / easily) answered the questions.

14. I am (truly / true) grateful for your help.

15. They (gentle / gently) carried the boxes of light bulbs.

Write the following sentence in three ways. Each time, put the adverb *easily* in a different place in the sentence.

I passed my driver's test.

16. _____

_____

17. _____

_____

18. _____

_____

Check your answers on page 155.

Practice

Underline each adverb. Then circle the word it describes.

19. Sam and Nancy woke up early on Saturday morning.

20. Their alarm clock buzzed suddenly.

21. They were very eager to start the day.

22. Quickly, they dressed and got some coffee.

23. They usually get to the first yard sale by nine o'clock.

24. Sellers often display their best products in the morning.

25. The women carefully look through piles of clothes.

26. They rarely end their day without a purchase.

Add an adverb to the sentences below.

27. Each day, airplanes fly _____ through the skies above.

28. Their engines roar _____ for all to hear.

29. The mayor gets _____ angry complaints from neighbors.

30. However, some residents _____ look forward to each plane's take–off and landing.

31. They are _____ entertained by the power of the jets.

32. These people _____ get tired of sitting on the grassy hill and waiting for a plane to fly over.

Rewrite each sentence using adverbs instead of adjectives.

33. The breeze is slow and gentle.

   _____

34. The dentist's work was careful and precise.

   _____

35. Mariah dresses in a colorful way.

   _____

36. The nurse spoke with a quiet, respectful voice.

   _____

Check your answers on page 155.

GED Skill Strategy

Proofreading for Grammar Errors

Mistakes, or errors, can make your writing difficult to read and understand and can distract your reader. Finding and fixing errors in writing is called proofreading.

 Strategy Look for errors in your writing. Follow these steps.

1. Read each sentence separately, slowly, and carefully.
2. Watch for the kinds of mistakes you have made in the past.
3. Think about what does not "sound" right as you read the sentences out loud or in your head.

Exercise 1: Read these sentences. Circle any errors.

1. The shipments needs to go out by noon today.
2. The shipping clerks brought they supplies to the floor.
3. He be the fastest worker out there now.
4. Some of the worker's think the pay is too low.
5. They don't move as quick as other workers.
6. Mrs. Vargas gives the employees's annual review.
7. All the clerks get his paycheck on Friday.
8. The accountant take tax deductions from their checks.
9. Mrs. Vargas done called the accountant today.
10. People respects Mrs. Vargas.

Exercise 2: List two types of grammar errors that you will watch out for after working through this unit.

_____

_____

_____

When you are correcting something you have written, you can use proofreading symbols to make your corrections.

 Strategy   Correct your errors. Follow these steps.

1. Use these symbols to make corrections:

    ~~cross out~~ Draw a line through an error. Write the correct word or words above.

    ^ Place this symbol where you want to insert a word or words.

    → Use an arrow to show where a word or words should be moved.

2. Make your corrections neatly and carefully.

Exercise 3: Are the changes correct? Write *yes* if they are and *no* if they are not.

1. The ~~childs~~ children on my block are getting older. _____

2. They ^have been growing quickly. _____

Exercise 4: Proofread these sentences. Use the symbols from the strategy above.

1. Edward, my business partner, love to cook.

2. Him brings me a delicious lunch every Friday.

3. He has did this ever since we teamed up together.

4. I pay five dollars for each one of Edwards's lunches.

5. I treat sometimes him to lunch at the corner diner.

6. These is just one reason why we like being business partners.

Check your answers on page 156.

Correcting Sentence Errors

Some questions on the GED Writing Test ask you to proofread the sentences for grammar errors. You must read a sentence and decide whether it has an error in grammar or usage. If a sentence has an error, you will have to choose the best correction.

To be successful, read each sentence carefully. Decide what the mistake is. Think about how you would correct the mistake. See if there is an answer choice that matches your correction.

 Strategy   Try this strategy with the example below. Use these steps.

Step 1   Read the sentence.

Step 2   Decide if the sentence has an error.

Step 3   If the sentence does have an error, think about how to correct the error.

Step 4   Find the answer choice that matches your correction. Some questions have the choice *(4) no correction is necessary*. Select that choice if there are no errors.

Example

All the mens' computers were broken.

(1)   change <u>mens'</u> to <u>men</u>

(2)   change <u>mens'</u> to <u>men's</u>

(3)   change <u>computers</u> to <u>computer's</u>

(4)   no correction is necessary

In Step 1 you read the sentence carefully. In Step 2 you decided that there was an error (*mens'*). In Step 3 you decided how to correct the error. In Step 4 you looked at the answer choices to see which one matched your correction. The correct answer is (2). The word *mens'* has an apostrophe error. *Men* is the plural form of *man*, so the correct possessive form of the word is *men's*.

Practice the strategy. Use the steps that you learned. Circle the number of the correct answer.

1. The parade was held tomorrow to honor our veterans.

   (1) change was to will be
   (2) change held to hold
   (3) change our to your
   (4) change veterans to veteran's

2. One of our veteran's, Manuel Davis, fought in two wars.

   (1) change veteran's to veterans
   (2) change Davis to davis
   (3) change fought to fighted
   (4) no correction is necessary

3. Some of his war stories are very sad.

   (1) change his to he
   (2) change stories to storys
   (3) change are to is
   (4) no correction is necessary

4. Those leg wound he got was serious.

   (1) change Those to That
   (2) change he to He
   (3) change got to gotten
   (4) change was to been

5. The streets of miami are filled with parade watchers.

   (1) change streets to Streets
   (2) change streets to street's
   (3) change miami to Miami
   (4) no correction is necessary

Check your answers on page 156.

Read each paragraph and question carefully. Circle the number of the correct answer.

Questions 1–4 refer to following paragraph.

(1) You can teach children about money. (2) Teach childs to save some of the money they earn. (3) Open a savings account and let them sees the balance grow. (4) Teach kids to hunt for values when shopping. (5) This children will learn to treat money with care and respect.

1. Which correction should be made to sentence 1?

    (1) change <u>You</u> to <u>Your</u>
    (2) change <u>teach</u> to <u>teaching</u>
    (3) change <u>children</u> to <u>child</u>
    (4) no correction is necessary

2. Which correction should be made to sentence 2?

    (1) change <u>childs</u> to <u>child</u>
    (2) change <u>childs</u> to <u>children</u>
    (3) change <u>money</u> to <u>monies</u>
    (4) no correction is necessary

3. Which correction should be made to sentence 3?

    (1) change <u>Open</u> to <u>Opening</u>
    (2) change <u>savings</u> to <u>Savings</u>
    (3) change <u>let</u> to <u>be letting</u>
    (4) change <u>sees</u> to <u>see</u>

4. Which correction should be made to sentence 5?

    (1) change <u>This</u> to <u>These</u>
    (2) change <u>learn</u> to <u>learns</u>
    (3) change <u>treat</u> to <u>treats</u>
    (4) no correction is necessary

Questions 5–8 refer to following paragraph.

(1) Movie theaters have became more than just a place to watch the latest blockbuster. (2) Now many theater's restaurants include everything from pizza to fine gourmet dining. (3) In some theaters today, people was playing video games, surfing the Internet, and watching trailers of upcoming films. (4) Next, might be doing laundry or even clothes shopping!

5. Which correction should be made to sentence 1?

(1) change theaters to theateres

(2) change have to has

(3) change became to become

(4) no correction is necessary

6. Which correction should be made to sentence 2?

(1) change theater's to theaters

(2) change theater's to theaters'

(3) change include to includes

(4) change fine to finely

7. Which correction should be made to sentence 3?

(1) change people to People

(2) change was to were

(3) change was to are

(4) no correction is necessary

8. Which correction should be made to sentence 4?

(1) change might to people might

(2) change be to is

(3) change doing to do

(4) change clothes to cloths

(1) The scene at Ralph's Roller Rink was exciting. (2) Teenagers were everywhere, laughing and talking loud on their cell phones. (3) The music blared, and young people pushed and shoved its way onto the rink.

9. Which correction should be made to sentence 2?

    (1) change Teenagers to Teenager's
    (2) change were to was
    (3) change loud to loudly
    (4) no correction is necessary

10. Which correction should be made to sentence 3?

    (1) change blared to blaring
    (2) change pushed to pushing
    (3) change its to their
    (4) change rink to Rink

Check your answers on page 157.

Unit Skill 1 Check-Up Chart

Check your answers. In the first column, circle the numbers of any questions that you missed. Then look across the rows to see the skills you need to review and the pages where you can find each skill.

Question	Skill	Page
1, 2	Nouns and Plurals	14–19
3	Subject–Verb Agreement	42–45
4	Adjectives	28–31
5	Verb Forms	32–37
6	Possessive Nouns	20–23
7	Helping Verbs	38–41
8	Parts of a Sentence	12–13
9	Adverbs	46–49
10	Pronouns	24–27

Unit 2 | Clear Sentences

parallel

fragment

series

clause

In this unit you will learn about

- complete sentences
- run-on sentences and fragments
- agreement between subjects and verbs
- parallel structure

Good writers use complete sentences to express their thoughts. Complete sentences make writing clear and easy to understand. Writers of books, magazine articles, and personal letters use complete sentences.

Think of the types of writing you do in your daily life. When do you use complete sentences?

_____

_____

Some types of writing do not require complete sentences. For example, to-do lists do not have to be written in complete sentences.

What else do you write that does not require complete sentences?

_____

_____

sentence
a group of words that contains a subject, a verb, and a complete thought

subject
the person, thing, or idea that a sentence is about

predicate
the words, including the verb, that tell what the subject is or does

In the cartoon, you can see that Henry is speaking in complete **sentences**. Frank is not. People often speak in incomplete sentences. When you talk, your gestures and your tone of voice help make your ideas clear.

When you write, however, the reader sees only your written words. This is why you should write in complete sentences.

As you learned in Unit 1, a complete sentence must express a complete thought. To do this, it needs a **subject** and a **predicate**. The subject identifies *who* or *what* the sentence is about. The predicate tells what the subject *is* or *does*. The predicate includes the verb.

Examples: Incomplete Sentences That Need a Subject

◼ Is going to the movies. (*Who* is going to the movies?)
◼ Will happen next year. (*What* will happen next year?)

Add a subject to make each incomplete sentence complete.

1. _____ is going to the movies.
2. _____ will happen next year.

Examples: Incomplete Sentences That Need a Predicate

◼ The large brown dog. (What does the dog *do*?)
◼ The dog's owners. (Who *are* they, or what do they *do*?)

Add a predicate to make each incomplete sentence complete.

3. The large brown dog _____ .
4. The dog's owners _____ .

Check your answers on page 157.

▶ **GED Tip**

When you write your GED Essay, make sure each sentence makes sense. Check that each sentence has a subject, a predicate, and a complete thought.

Circle the subject and underline the predicate in these sentences.

1. (Maria) writes to her parents every week.

2. Her parents wait for those letters.

3. Her letters are important to them.

4. She writes about her job most of the time.

5. She tells them about her friends sometimes.

6. They miss her.

Find the verbs in the sentences above. Write them below.

7. (1) _____   10. (4) _____

8. (2) _____   11. (5) _____

9. (3) _____   12. (6) _____

Rewrite the following groups of words to make complete sentences.

13. works very hard

_____

_____

14. the high school student

_____

_____

15. studied all weekend

_____

_____

16. a flock of pigeons

_____

_____

Check your answers on page 157.

run-on sentence
two or more complete thoughts that are written together without correct punctuation

independent clause
a group of words that can stand alone as a sentence

In a **run-on sentence**, the words run on too long. The writer links together more than one complete sentence. Separate ideas should be placed in separate sentences.

Examples: Run-on Sentences

- I can't believe I ate the whole thing it was delicious.
- The bill was very popular among the farmers back home the senator voted for it.
- The table is a square it has four equal sides.

Look back at the examples and draw a slash mark (/) where you think a sentence should end.

Each of the examples above has two complete ideas. Each example contains two **independent clauses**. Each example can be divided into two sentences.

- I can't believe I ate the whole thing! It was delicious!
- The bill was very popular among the farmers back home. The senator voted for it.

You can also keep the words in a single sentence. In this case, you separate the independent clauses with a semicolon.

- The table is a square; it has four equal sides.

Write these run-on sentences as correct sentences.

1. Tigers are cats they have stripes.

_____

2. The dress came in three colors I liked the blue one best.

_____

_____

3. I go to work then I come home.

_____

Check your answers on page 157.

To write well, you need to know the difference between a sentence and a **sentence fragment**. This is not always easy to know. Some sentence fragments are long and look like sentences.

sentence fragment
a group of words that is not a sentence

For example, answers to the questions *when?* or *why?* often begin with the words *while, before, after,* and *because*. These answers are not sentences. They are sentence fragments.

Examples: Sentence Fragments

- Because it was five o'clock.
- While she was working days at the restaurant.

Now, read these sentences:

- I left work.
- Mary went to school at night.

Both of the fragments above are longer than the sentences. However, the sentences sound more complete.

There are two ways to make the fragments above into sentences.

- Add the fragment to a complete sentence.
- Take out the first word of the fragment.

Your choice depends on how much information you want to include. The first way combines the fragments with the sentences.

- Because it was five o'clock, I left work.
- While she was working days at the restaurant, Mary went to school at night.

You could also combine the fragments and sentences this way:

- I left work because it was five o'clock.
- Mary went to school at night while she was working days at the restaurant.

The second way to turn some fragments into sentences is to take out the first word. These are complete sentences:

- It was five o'clock.
- She was working days at the restaurant.

This method will not turn all fragments into sentences. You know you have a sentence if you have both a subject and a predicate. *It* and *She* are the subjects of the examples above. The remaining words of each sentence are the predicates.

Another kind of fragment begins with a word ending in *-ing*. This is a fragment:

- Going to school at night.

This kind of fragment is fixed in a different way. Add a subject and a **helping verb** to make it a sentence.

- Mary is going to school at night.

In this example, only a subject and a helping verb were added. You could also lengthen the sentence by adding other words:

- Mary is going to school at night to get her GED.

helping verb
a verb like *have, be,* and *do* that is used with other verbs

Make these fragments into sentences.

1. Answering questions

   _____

2. Following me

   _____

3. After I had supper

   _____

4. Hoping for rain

   _____

5. When I got home

   _____

Check your answers on page 158.

> **GED Tip**
>
> You can usually tell a sentence fragment by the way that it sounds. A fragment does not state a complete thought. It may not make sense. Avoid using sentence fragments when writing your GED Essay.

Write these run-on sentences as correct sentences.

1. Her car broke down she called the garage.

   _____

   _____

2. There are nine planets in the solar system the one closest to the sun is Mercury.

   _____

   _____

Add words to change these sentence fragments into sentences.

3. Before I could say a word.

   _____

   _____

4. Loves pizza.

   _____

   _____

Take out words to change these sentence fragments into sentences.

5. After they went home.

   _____

6. Because I left the window open.

   _____

Add a subject and a helping verb to make these fragments into sentences.

7. Building shelves.

   _____

8. Talking on the telephone.

   _____

Check your answers on page 158.

compound subject
two or more subjects, usually joined by *and* or *or*

Compound subjects are usually joined with the word *and*.

- ■ Ling <u>and</u> Taneeka make a good team.
- ■ Reading <u>and</u> writing are important skills.

When two parts of a compound subject are linked with the word *and*, the subject is always plural. When other linking words are used, such as *or*, the subject can be either plural or singular. Compound subjects are linked with one of the following words or sets of words.

- ■ and
- ■ or
- ■ either . . . or
- ■ neither . . . nor
- ■ not only . . . but (also)

When the compound subject isn't linked with *and*, the verb matches the part of the subject that is closest to it.

Examples: Compound Subjects

- ■ Ling or <u>Taneeka</u> (is) making dinner tonight.
- ■ Neither Ling nor <u>Taneeka</u> (is) at work now.
- ■ Not only reading but also <u>writing</u> (is) an important skill.

Notice the verbs in the next pair of sentences.

- ■ Either the newspaper or the magazines <u>are</u> on the table.
- ■ Either the magazines or the newspaper <u>is</u> on the table.

Both sentences have the same compound subjects. Both sets of subjects are linked with *either . . . or*, but different forms of the verb are used. In the first sentence, the plural verb *are* matches *magazines*, the part of the subject closest to the verb. In the second sentence, the singular verb *is* matches *newspaper*, the part of the subject closest to the verb.

Underline the correct form of the verb in parentheses to complete each sentence.

1. Either the driver or the assistants (plan / plans) to load the truck.

2. Not only bricks but also logs (is / are) being shipped.

3. Julio and Jennie (want / wants) to drive the truck.

4. Either the assistants or the receptionist (need / needs) to sign for the package.

5. Not only paper but also pencils (is / are) being handed out before the meeting.

6. Neither Paul nor Kiri (expect / expects) to be late.

Remember the different ways that compound subjects can be linked. Watch out for sentences that seem to have compound subjects but really don't. The following two sentences are correct. Both have singular subjects. The words set off by commas are not part of the subjects. They do not affect the verbs.

Underline the subject and circle the verb in each sentence.

7. His wife, not his children, is from California.

8. The manager, as well as all of her employees, attends the meetings.

Underline the correct form of the verb in parentheses to complete each sentence.

9. My family, including my sister-in-law, (is / are) coming for dinner.

10. His son, but not his daughter, (walk / walks) to school.

11. Stella, as well as Mae, (hope / hopes) for a raise.

12. Isaac, not Mariana and Paul, (want / wants) to be a teacher.

Check your answers on page 158.

In some sentences, the subject comes after the verb. Some of these sentences begin with *Here* or *There*; others begin with a phrase telling where something is.

Circle the subjects in each sentence.

1. Here is the letter.

2. There are three pages.

3. In front of it is an envelope.

4. At the back are order forms.

5. Where is their earlier order?

6. Here it is.

7. At the top is the date.

8. There is no signature.

Circle the subject in each sentence. Then underline the correct form of the verb in parentheses.

9. In our garden (grow / grows) all kinds of vegetables.

10. Across the street (live / lives) two young couples.

11. Around the corner (stand / stands) a statue of Booker T. Washington.

12. Here (is / are) your change.

13. There (go / goes) the mail carriers.

14. On the next block (is / are) a shopping center.

15. There (is / are) many stores.

16. In each of them (work / works) at least one person.

Check your answers on page 158.

GED Tip

The key to making sure verbs agree with subjects is finding the subject. On the GED Writing Test, make this your first step after reading through a sentence.

Underline the correct verb to complete each sentence.

1. Across the hall (is / are) two vacant apartments.

2. There (is / are) many reasons why you might want to move in.

3. Down the street from us (live / lives) two little girls with whom your daughter could play.

4. I don't think the apartment (need / needs) to be painted.

5. The union president, not the members, (meet / meets) with management.

6. Labor and management (work / works) together to reach an agreement.

7. Not only the members but also Jimmy (was / were) glad when it was all over.

8. The tacos and the tamales (look / looks) good.

9. Either soup or salad (come / comes) with the dinner.

10. Neither her son nor her daughters (has / have) any cavities.

11. The chicken, but not the potatoes, (is / are) cooked enough.

12. The tennis player and her coach (meet / meets) every day.

13. Daily practice (is / are) very important.

14. Either a pencil or two pens (is / are) on the desk.

15. Neither pens nor a pencil (is / are) on the table.

16. Jake, as well as his three children, (like/ likes) to rent videos.

17. The children, but not Jake, (enjoy / enjoys) cartoons.

18. Jake (prefer / prefers) action and adventure movies.

Check your answers on page 158.

series
a group of three or more words or phrases joined by commas and *and* or *or*

parallel structure
all words or phrases of a series in the same form

Sometimes three or more nouns, verbs, adjectives, or phrases are joined in a sentence. These words are connected with commas and a joining word such as *and* or *or*. These connected words are called a **series**.

Example: Her apartment is <u>small</u>, <u>neat</u>, and <u>clean</u>.

All the items in a series must be in the same form. A series in the correct form is said to be in **parallel structure**. Look at the series below. What is incorrect in the series?

Example: Not Parallel Structure

■ The mail attendant's job is to sort, to deliver, and collecting the mail.

The first two verbs, *to sort* and *to deliver*, are in the same form. The last verb, *collecting*, is not in the same form as the other two.

Example: Parallel Structure

■ The mail attendant's job is to sort, to deliver, and to collect the mail.

Now all three verbs are in the same form.

Underline the three items in the series. Then write *P* if the sentence is in parallel structure and *NP* if it is not in parallel structure.

1. The rap singer has wealth, talent, and is famous.

   _____

2. Fame can be exciting, rewarding, and it can be a challenge.

   _____

3. We dined, danced, and stayed out until midnight.

   _____

Check your answers on page 159.

GED Tip

Whenever you write a series in a sentence, check that all of the items use parallel structure.

Underline the three items in each series. Then write *P* if the sentence is in parallel structure and *NP* if it is not in parallel structure.

1. Most companies today want employees with different backgrounds, ideas, and skills. _____

2. Executives, managers, and hourly workers all need to get along with people different from themselves. _____

3. Diversity in the workplace is important, useful, and being exciting. _____

4. My cousin, my father, and my sister all work for Union Industries. _____

5. Union Industries is a growing, smart, and differently company. _____

6. This company holds workshops regularly, eagerly, and convenient. _____

Cross out the item in each series that is not parallel in structure. Write the correct form of the item that is not parallel in the blank. If the sentence structure is parallel, write *P* in the blank.

7. The parking policy in this neighborhood is unfairly, annoying, and disrespectful to the residents. _____

8. Homeowners, renters, and landlords all have complained to city officials. _____

9. They complained loudly, often, and angry. _____

10. People from outside the city come here, park their cars, and leaving their trash everywhere! _____

11. City officials plan to hold a meeting, hear residents' ideas, and be planning a new parking policy. _____

12. They are asking residents to make their comments respectful, brief, and clearly. _____

Check your answers on page 159.

GED Skill Strategy

Writing Complete and Correct Sentences

To be complete, a sentence must have a subject, a predicate, and a complete thought.

> **Strategy** Plan what you write. Follow these steps.
> 1. Plan the subject and the predicate.
> 2. Ask yourself: <u>Who</u> or <u>What</u> is doing something? What is he or she <u>doing</u>?

Exercise 1: Read the paragraph. Underline the sentence fragments. Then write the fragments as complete sentences.

Ed and I are thinking about moving to Des Moines. Offered a job there. At a radio station. A good opportunity. The job offers a higher salary. Probably will take it. One of the things we want to check before we move is the school system. Want the kids to have a good school. Ed hopes the high school has a good football team. Our son Paul starting at quarterback.

1. _____

_____

2. _____

_____

3. _____

_____

4. _____

_____

5. _____

_____

6. _____

_____

Run-on sentences and sentence fragments make writing confusing to read. Correct these errors in your writing.

 Strategy Always reread what you write. Follow these steps.

1. If you find run-on sentences, rewrite them.
2. If you find fragments, make them into complete sentences.

Exercise 2: Underline the sentence fragments and circle the run-on sentences in this paragraph.

Went to the company's Human Resource Department yesterday. Because I just got married. Want to extend my medical coverage to my wife. I have to fill out some forms then I have to wait thirty days for insurance to take effect. Not too expensive. It is a good deal I am happy.

Exercise 3: Rewrite the paragraph. Change the fragments and run-on sentences into sentences.

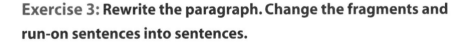

_____

_____

_____

_____

_____

_____

_____

_____

Check your answers on page 159.

Revising Sentence Errors

On the GED Writing Test, some questions have a sentence with a part underlined. The answer choices will give possible ways to revise the underlined part of the sentence to make it correct. The first answer choice is always the same as the original underlined part.

When you see a sentence revision question, first decide if the underlined words are correct. If they are not, skim the answer choices to see which choice is the correct way to rewrite the sentence.

 Strategy Try this strategy with the following example. Use these steps.

Step 1 Read the sentence.

Step 2 Pay attention to the underlined words.

Step 3 If the underlined words are correct, choose option (1).

Step 4 If the underlined words are not correct, skim the answer choices to find the correct version.

Example

What is the best way to rewrite the underlined portion of the sentence? If the original is the best way, choose option (1).

Jim and Andy <u>seems angry</u>.

    (1) seems angry

    (2) seems angrily

    (3) seem angry

    (4) seeming angry

In Step 1 you read the sentence carefully. In Step 2 you studied the underlined words, *seems angry*. In Step 3 you realized that these words were not correct as written. In Step 4 you found the verb form that agrees with the plural subject *Jim and Andy*. Choice (3) is correct. The verb *seem* agrees with the plural subject: *Jim and Andy seem angry*.

Circle the number of the best way to rewrite the underlined portion of each sentence. If the original is the best way, choose option (1).

1. American adults <u>feel sad, lonely, and depression</u> about three times per month, a study shows.

   (1) feel sad, lonely, and depression
   (2) feel sadly, lonely, and depression
   (3) feel sad, lonely, and depressed
   (4) feeling sad, lonely, and depression

2. Depressed people are less <u>healthy they often smoke</u>.

   (1) healthy they often smoke
   (2) healthy. They often smoke
   (3) healthy they often smoked
   (4) healthy they often be smoking

3. They also <u>does not exercise often</u>.

   (1) does not exercise often
   (2) does not exercise oftenly
   (3) does not exercising often
   (4) do not exercise often

4. Women report more "down" <u>days. Than men</u> report.

   (1) days. Than men
   (2) day's. Than men
   (3) days than men
   (4) days, than men

5. Either a talk with a friend or some simple exercises <u>help keep your</u> mood positive.

   (1) help keep your
   (2) helps keep your
   (3) helps keeping your
   (4) helps keep you're

Check your answers on page 160.

Read each paragraph and question carefully. Circle the number of the correct answer.

Questions 1–3 are based on the following paragraph.

(1) Voters in this country have <u>rights. (2) When they</u> cast their ballots. (3) Voters must be able to mark their ballot in privacy. (4) <u>Have the right</u> to stay in the voting booth for up to five minutes. (5) Poll workers or even a <u>friend are allowed to help</u> you cast your ballot.

1. Which revision should be made to the underlined portion of sentences 1 and 2? If the original is the best way, choose option (1).

   (1) rights. When they
   (2) rights. When their
   (3) rights when they
   (4) right's. When they

2. Which revision should be made to the underlined portion of sentence 4? If the original is the best way, choose option (1).

   (1) Have the right
   (2) Has the right
   (3) Had the right
   (4) Voters have the right

3. Which revision should be made to the underlined portion of sentence 5? If the original is the best way, choose option (1).

   (1) friend are allowed to help
   (2) friend is allowed to help
   (3) friend be allowed to help
   (4) friend are allowing to help

Questions 4–7 are based on the following paragraph.

(1) Childcare providers need to be smart, kind, and <u>having energy.</u> (2) They work mostly with <u>children they also work</u> with parents. (3) The <u>classroom has all kinds</u> of opportunities to teach adults as well as kids. (4) For example, <u>there is</u> parenting tips on the bulletin board right alongside children's artwork.

4. Which revision should be made to the underlined portion of sentence 1? If the original is the best way, choose option (1).

    (1) having energy
    (2) had energy
    (3) has energy
    (4) energetic

5. Which revision should be made to the underlined portion of sentence 2? If the original is the best way, choose option (1).

    (1) children they also work
    (2) children. They also work
    (3) children they also working
    (4) children they also worked

6. Which revision should be made to the underlined portion of sentence 3? If the original is the best way, choose option (1).

    (1) classroom has all kinds
    (2) classroom have all kinds
    (3) classroom be all kinds
    (4) classroom being all kinds

7. Which revision should be made to the underlined portion of sentence 4? If the original is the best way, choose option (1).

    (1) there is
    (2) they're is
    (3) their is
    (4) there are

Questions 8–9 are based on the following paragraph.

(1) The night manager's job requirements are posted here. (2) So that all employees can see them. (3) The night manager is responsible for counting money, serving customers, and to close the store at 10:00.

8. Which revision should be made to the underlined portion of sentences 1 and 2? If the original is the best way, choose option (1).

   (1) here. So that all employees
   (2) hear. So that all employees
   (3) here. So that all employee's
   (4) here so that all employees

9. Which revision should be made to the underlined portion of sentence 3? If the original is the best way, choose option (1).

   (1) to close
   (2) to closes
   (3) closing
   (4) to closed

Check your answers on page 160.

Unit 2 Skill Check-Up Chart

Check your answers. In the first column, circle the numbers of any questions that you missed. Then look across the rows to see the skills you need to review and the pages where you can find each skill.

Question	Skill	Page
1, 2	Sentences That make Sense	58–59
5, 8	Run-on Sentences and Fragments	60–63
3, 6, 7	More on Subject and Verb Agreement	64–67
4, 9	Parallel Structure	68–69

Unit 3

Capitalization, Punctuation, and Spelling

In this unit you will learn about

- capitalizing in sentences
- capitalizing days, dates, and names
- punctuating sentence endings
- using commas
- using apostrophes and quotation marks
- spelling words that sound alike
- correcting misspelled words

apostrophe

homonym

conjunction

comma

Correct capitalization, punctuation, and spelling are important to good writing. If your writing has mistakes in these areas, it will be difficult to read and understand. Learning some basic rules can help you to avoid common mistakes.

Write one example of when you use capital letters.

_____

List two punctuation marks that you know. When do you use each one?

_____

_____

capitalize
to write with a
capital letter

specific
exact, definite

When do you **capitalize** the first letter of a word? Here are three rules to follow.

Rule 1:   Capitalize the first letter of a word that begins a sentence.

Example:

■ This cat is mine.

Rule 2:   Always capitalize the word *I*.

Examples:

■ I, I'll, I've

Rule 3:   Capitalize the **specific** name of a person, place, or thing.

Examples:

■ Jane, Chicago, Congress, Big Town Supermarket

Read the note. Then circle the letters that should be capitalized.

pat,

    i will help you choose a birthday present for maria.
let's meet at franklin's video store tomorrow. i'm sure
we can find a movie your sister will like.

leslie

Rewrite the note with correct capitalization.

_____

_____

_____

_____

_____

Check your answers on page 161.

Some writers capitalize incorrectly. They capitalize every word they think is important. When you write, don't capitalize just to **emphasize** something.

emphasize
to make important

Examples: Incorrect Capitalization

- Mac has a Job at a Restaurant in the City.
  (incorrect capitals: *job, restaurant, city*)
- He takes the Bus to his Hockey game each Week.
  (incorrect capitals: *bus, hockey, week*)

Read the note. Then circle the letters that are incorrectly capitalized.

Dear Ms. Rivera,

Lucy was Home sick for a Week with the Measles. Her Friend Roger brought over the Homework Assignments and told her what happened in School. I think Lucy is Up To Date in her Schoolwork.

Mina Jones

Rewrite the note with correct capitalization.

_____

_____

_____

_____

_____

_____

_____

 GED Tip

Using capital letters too often is a much more common error than forgetting to capitalize. If there is not a rule for using a capital letter, do not use one.

Check your answers on page 161.

When you write, remember to capitalize the first word in a sentence, the word *I*, and specific names.

When you are writing a title, always capitalize the first and last words of the title. Capitalize all other words except minor words like *of*, *and*, *to*, *for*, and *the*.

Examples:

- Every night, she watches *Wheel of Fortune*.
- Ernest Hemingway wrote *The Old Man and the Sea*.
- Two popular movies produced by George Lucas are *Star Wars: Revenge of the Sith* and *Indiana Jones and the Last Crusade*.

Rewrite the sentences with correct capitalization.

1. My son's favorite book is *green eggs and ham*.

_____

_____

2. He also loves *where the wild things are*.

_____

_____

3. *I love lucy* is an old TV show that is still popular.

_____

_____

4. My family loves the movie *butch cassidy and the sundance kid*.

_____

_____

Check your answers on page 161.

Practice

Each sentence below has one mistake in capitalization. Rewrite the sentences and correct the mistakes.

1. I did my best, and i got the job.

_____

_____

2. I thought the *Lord of the rings* movies were good.

_____

_____

3. tim took his son Adam to the clinic.

_____

_____

4. Wilma told me You fixed the leaky faucet.

_____

_____

5. We watch *The Young And the Restless* every afternoon.

_____

_____

6. we are going to a party tomorrow night.

_____

_____

7. She asked me if i'd bring my famous pasta salad.

_____

_____

Check your answers on page 161.

The months of the year begin with a capital letter.

Examples:

■ January, February, March, April, May, June, July, August, September, October, November, December

The days of the week begin with a capital letter.

Examples:

■ Sunday, Monday, Tuesday, Wednesday, Thursday, Friday, Saturday

The names of specific holidays begin with a capital letter.

Examples:

■ Ramadan, Thanksgiving, New Year's Eve, Yom Kippur, Memorial Day, the Fourth of July, Cinco de Mayo

However, the seasons are not capitalized.

Examples:

■ spring, summer, autumn (fall), winter

Words such as *today*, *tomorrow*, and *yesterday* aren't capitalized either.

Answer the questions. Write complete sentences using correct capitalization.

1. What is today's date?

   _____

2. What day of the week is today?

   _____

3. What holiday is nearest to today's date?

   _____

Check your answers on page 161.

GED Tip

When deciding whether to use a capital letter on the GED Writing Test, ask yourself, "Is this a specific day, date, or holiday?" If the answer is yes, capitalize.

Practice

Rewrite each sentence with correct capitalization.

1. Her Birthday is February 14, which is also Valentine's day.

   _____

   _____

2. Christmas Eve is on december 24, the day before christmas.

   _____

   _____

3. July is usually the hottest month of the Summer.

   _____

   _____

4. The weekend starts Tomorrow, on saturday.

   _____

   _____

5. Last year Columbus Day was on Monday, october 18.

   _____

   _____

6. My vacation begins on saturday, June 11, 2005.

   _____

   _____

7. Last year thanksgiving came on Thursday, November 26.

   _____

   _____

Check your answers on page 162.

People's names begin with capital letters. Capitalize first, middle, and last names, as well as initials. If a man's name includes *Jr.*, that is also capitalized.

John F. Kennedy

Susan B. Anthony

Dr. Martin Luther King, Jr.

title
a word used before a person's name, such as *Mrs.* or *Dr.*

relationship
a connection that is often personal

Capitalize **titles** such as *Mr., Mrs., Ms., Miss, Dr.*, and *Rev.* For example:

■ Rev. Darrel Berg, Dr. Maria Alvarez, Ms. Mary Lin

Do not capitalize a title that describes someone's job or a person's **relationship** to you. For example:

■ I made an appointment for my father with my doctor.

Here, the words *father* and *doctor* are not specific names of individuals. Therefore, they are not capitalized.

Sometimes at work you are asked for information to be used in an emergency.

Write the names of a relative or close friend and your doctor or clinic. Use full names and titles.

Person to notify
in case of emergency: _____

Doctor or clinic: _____

Check your answers on page 162.

In an address, capitalize the following:

- the name of a street
- the words *Street, Drive, Road, Avenue, Lane*
- the words *Suite, Apartment,* and *Unit*
- the name of a city, state, county, and country

Dr. Judy Myers
3001 Lexington Road
Baltimore, MD 20018

Mr. Jerry McCord
1800 Marshall Street, Suite 121
Lincoln, NE 68505

Examples:

- They moved to Billings, Montana, in the United States.
- The schools in Montgomery County are excellent.
- I live at 8 Knoll Road in Toronto, Canada.

Notice that the word *the* isn't capitalized when it's part of the name of a country.

- the United States

Write a sentence using your street address.

Every state has a two-letter abbreviation. Both letters are capitalized. The two-letter abbreviation is used when addressing letters. It is also correct to write out the state name. For example:

- San Antonio, TX or San Antonio, Texas

Write the name of your city and state both ways.

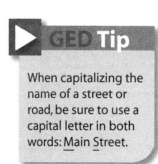

GED Tip

When capitalizing the name of a street or road, be sure to use a capital letter in both words: Main Street.

Check your answers on page 162.

return address
the address a letter comes from

Address this envelope to a friend. Include your full return address in the upper left corner. Use two-letter abbreviations for the states.

the Rocky Mountains

_____

_____

_____

           _____

           _____

           _____

the Empire State Building

Capitalize the names of specific rivers, lakes, bays, parks, mountain ranges, and buildings. For example:

■ We saw the <u>C</u>olorado <u>R</u>iver and the <u>R</u>ocky <u>M</u>ountains.

The words *river, bay, lake, park, mountain,* and *building* aren't capitalized if they aren't part of the name of a specific place. For example:

■ We saw the river and the mountains.

Write a sentence about a specific place (river, lake, bay, park, mountain, or building) you've visited.

_____

_____

Rewrite the sentence without using the specific name of the place.

_____

_____

Lake Champlain

Check your answers on page 162.

Practice

Each sentence below has two mistakes in capitalization. Rewrite the sentences and correct the mistakes.

1. I took my mother to see a Doctor in Baltimore, maryland.

_____

_____

2. My sister, dr. Roberta P. Wong, works at the Hospital.

_____

_____

3. Mr. Martinez showed miss foster how to fill out her time card.

_____

_____

4. Roger's minister is Rev. calvin franklin.

_____

_____

5. Please send the bill to ms. Marilyn Stuart, 6701 Lincoln street, Portland, ME.

_____

_____

6. Tourists love to visit the White House and the washington monument in Washington, D.C.

_____

_____

7. On their vacation, Mr. and Mrs. Mitzner saw The Grand Canyon, Yellowstone National park, and two state parks.

_____

_____

Check your answers on page 162.

Knowing What to Capitalize

Capitalization is important in good writing. It makes writing clearer and easier to read.

 Train your eyes to look for specific names. Follow these steps.
1. Look for *I* and look for specific names and titles.
2. Notice where sentences start.

Exercise 1: Circle the words that should be capitalized.

i've decided i should return to texas to be closer to my parents. my wife barbara agrees. we will be happier there than we have been in kansas. we will probably live in dallas or perhaps in houston.

Exercise 2: Rewrite these sentences with correct capitalization.

i come from ho chi minh city in the south of vietnam. It used to be called Saigon. now I live in canada. I moved with my family to toronto. it is the capital of the province of ontario. it is a nice city, and i like it very much.

_____
_____
_____
_____
_____
_____
_____
_____

Toronto

It is also important to know which words are not capitalized. Words that are not specific names of people, places, or things should not be capitalized.

 Strategy Be careful not to capitalize incorrectly. Follow these steps.

1. Reread what you wrote.

2. If you capitalized a word that is not a specific name or the beginning of a sentence, remove the capital letter.

Exercise 3: Circle the words in the paragraph that are incorrectly capitalized.

The Salton Sea is a shallow Salt Lake about 370 square miles in area. It is located in California. It was formed by the flooding of the Colorado River. The River flooded around the Year 1905.

Exercise 4: Rewrite the paragraph with correct capitalization.

in 1891 the Famous scientist Marie curie went to paris, France, to study Chemistry and physics. She came from poland. She and her Husband, Pierre, discovered the element radium. Marie Curie was the first person to be awarded the nobel Prize twice.

Marie Curie

Check your answers on page 162.

punctuation marks
symbols used in writing to make the meaning of sentences clear

state
to say in words

statement
a sentence that gives information and facts

A sentence always ends with a **punctuation mark**. This can be a period, a question mark, or an exclamation point.

The punctuation mark used most often is the period. It ends sentences that give information and **state** facts. This kind of sentence is called a **statement**.

Examples:

- My name is Geraldo.
- I have two older sisters.
- We live in Ohio.

A question mark shows that the sentence is a question. A question asks for information.

Examples:

- What are you doing after work?
- Do you want to see a movie?
- Should we eat dinner before we see the movie?

An exclamation point shows excitement. Think about what happens when you are excited, scared, or angry. You might shout out a word or a very short sentence.

Examples:

- Hooray!
- Watch out!
- Get out of my way!

You could win

$10,000,000!

Enter the contest today!

Act now!

Advertisers use exclamation points to try to get you excited about their products.

Write three sentences: one that makes a statement, one that asks a question, and one that shows excitement.

1. _____

2. _____

3. _____

Check your answers on page 163.

Add periods, question marks, or exclamation points where needed in the groups of words below.

1. I ran an ad in the newspaper

2. It looked like it would be easy to get a job

3. At work I type, file, and answer the phone

4. This is really an amazing surprise

5. Did my husband help you plan the party

6. This is an emergency

7. Is she all right

8. You were asleep when your mother called

9. How many planets are in the solar system

10. Is the moon a planet

11. Moons are not considered planets

12. Some planets have more than one moon

13. Jupiter has several moons

14. What is a hacksaw

15. A hacksaw cuts through metal

16. Do you know the differences among a hacksaw, a crosscut saw, and a ripsaw

Check your answers on page 163.

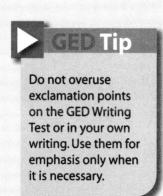

GED Tip

Do not overuse exclamation points on the GED Writing Test or in your own writing. Use them for emphasis only when it is necessary.

Lesson 18   Using Commas

pause
to stop briefly

set off
to separate

Commas tell the reader when to **pause** while reading a sentence. Commas are used in lists, to **set off** things, and to add information.

Use a comma to separate three or more items in a list. The list can be of people, actions, places, things, or anything else.

Examples:

- Marla, Bill, Ed, Barbara, and I went to the game.
- Walter plans to paint the house, trim the trees, fix the roof, and clean the gutters.

Sometimes items in a list are connected with the word *or*.

Examples:

- We could eat lunch, go shopping, <u>or</u> see a movie.
- Will Robert, Nina, <u>or</u> Anna need the car today?

When you write a list as part of a sentence, put a comma after every item except the last in the list. Be sure to put a comma before the word *and* or *or*. Never put a comma after the word *and* or *or* in this kind of sentence.

Commas can change the meaning of a sentence. Pay attention to the commas in the sentences below.

- They serve pizza, roast, beef sandwiches, and salads.
- They serve pizza, roast beef, sandwiches, and salads.
- They serve pizza, roast beef sandwiches, and salads.

When you take notes, use commas to separate items in a list.

Suppose the restaurant serves only three things. Which sentence is correctly punctuated? Only the last sentence lists three items.

Look at the following sentences. The only difference in the way they are written are two commas. However, the meaning is different. The first sentence is about two people, and the second sentence is about three people.

- Mary Ann and James are having a party.
- Mary, Ann, and James are having a party.

Supply the missing commas in this sentence.

The seven continents are Asia Africa North America South America Europe Australia and Antarctica.

You also use commas to set off words and phrases that describe nouns in your sentences. These descriptive phrases often start with the words *who* and *which*.

Examples:

- My brother, who is a student, can't afford to come this year.
- Her dog, a collie, is like a member of the family.
- The corner house, which is for sale, belongs to my aunt.

Take away the information between the commas and you still have complete sentences.

- My brother can't afford to come this year.
- Her dog is like a member of the family.
- The corner house belongs to my aunt.

The commas are used on both sides of the phrase to show that you are interrupting the sentence to give more information.

Information that is set off is not always found in the middle of a sentence. Such information may be placed at the end of a sentence.

Examples:

- Last year we visited my cousin, who is a student at the University of Texas.
- We ate at Le Bistro, an inexpensive French restaurant.
- Have you ever been to the Grand Canyon, one of the natural wonders of the world?

Names, short exclamations, and words like *yes* and *no* are often set off from the rest of a sentence with commas. This happens when such words come at the beginning, middle, or end of the sentence.

Check your answer on page 163.

In the last sentence below, there are commas on both sides of the word *Jessie*. This is because it appears in the middle of the sentence.

Examples:

- Hey, how are you?
- I hope to see you again, Tom.
- I told you, Jessie, we'll always be friends.

conjuction

a connecting word such as *and*, *but*, *or*, and *so* used with a comma to connect two complete thoughts

When two complete thoughts are joined with a **conjunction**, separate the two ideas with a comma.

Example:

- My rent is due Monday, and it can't be late again.

Be careful not to use a comma every time you see a conjunction. Use a comma only when the sentence contains two complete thoughts.

Example: Incorrect Comma

- Tomoko rang the buzzer, and waited for an answer. (*Waited for an answer* is not a complete thought.)

Example: Correct Comma

- Tomoko rang the buzzer, and she waited for an answer. (The comma after *buzzer* is correct. The conjunction *and* is now joining two complete thoughts.)

Decide whether each sentence contains two complete thoughts. If a comma is necessary, write C and insert the comma. Write NC if no comma is necessary.

GED Tip

Remember that a complete thought requires a subject and a verb. Use a comma to separate two complete thoughts joined by a conjunction.

1. Myra's job has good pay and full benefits. _____

2. She applied in May and got the job in July. _____

3. Myra received a good review and she was promised a raise. _____

Check your answers on page 163.

Add commas where needed to the sentences below.

1. The Declaration of Independence discusses life liberty and the pursuit of happiness.

2. Michael Phelps who is an American swimmer won eight medals in the 2004 Olympics.

3. I saw lions tigers and bears at the zoo.

4. Yes the Sears Tower is in Chicago.

5. Fluffy my kitten is Siamese.

6. I met Jason Kidd the famous basketball player.

7. Would you prefer coffee tea or milk?

8. Aaron I need you to clean your room.

9. We went shopping yesterday but we didn't buy anything.

10. Natalie who is rarely sick has a doctor's appointment.

11. Tanya who is my eldest niece is getting married.

12. She asked me to be her matron of honor and I agreed.

13. Tanya's mother my sister Janice will plan the wedding.

14. She will send the invitations and prepare the food.

15. The guests will include the couple's families friends and co-workers.

16. Tanya's fiancé Terrence is a cable installer.

17. They will live in Terrence's apartment but they hope to own a home someday.

18. I wish them health happiness and a long life together.

Check your answers on page 164.

Lesson 19　Using Apostrophes and Quotation Marks

contraction
two words joined together to form one word

An apostrophe (') is used to form a **contraction**. A contraction is two words combined into one. The apostrophe is used to take the place of a missing letter or letters.

Examples:

- I am ⟶ I'm
- I will ⟶ I'll
- I would ⟶ I'd
- you are ⟶ you're

- it is ⟶ it's
- would not ⟶ wouldn't
- does not ⟶ doesn't
- he would ⟶ he'd

When you make a contraction, be sure to put the apostrophe in the correct place.

Example: Incorrect Apostrophe Placement

- The mail carrier <u>does'nt</u> know the address.
  (No letter is missing between *does* and *not*.)

Example: Correct Apostrophe Placement

- The mail carrier <u>doesn't</u> know the address.
  (The apostrophe takes the place of the *o* in *not*.)

Read the following paragraph from a campaign speech.

It is time that the people of this state look closely at each candidate. I am the only one who would be a good governor. If elected, I will lower taxes and reduce unemployment. I will encourage industry to build factories here. My opponent cannot promise this. You are the voters; you will make the difference in this election.

Rewrite the paragraph with as many contractions as possible.

_____

_____

_____

_____

_____

_____

Check your answer on page 164.

An apostrophe is also used with nouns to show possession, or ownership. You may remember this from your work in Unit 1.

Examples:

- We watched the game on Harry's TV.
  (The TV belongs to Harry.)
- Elaine borrowed Mabel's sweater.
  (The sweater belongs to Mabel.)

Never use an apostrophe with a pronoun to show possession or ownership.

Example: Incorrect Apostrophe

- The book on the desk is her's.
  (No apostrophe is used in the possessive pronoun.)

Example: Correct Apostrophe

- The book on the desk is hers.

Underline the correct form of the word in parentheses to complete each sentence.

1. Bert launders the (teams / team's) uniforms.

2. The crew cleans the (arenas's / arena's) floor.

3. The team gets a good (night's / nights) sleep.

4. Tomorrow is the (coach's / coaches) big day.

5. The championship will be (our's / ours).

6. The (crowd's / crowds) cheers will be deafening.

7. Players hope the victory will be (theirs / their's).

8. These stadium tickets are (your's / yours).

9. The (rookies / rookie's) basket won the game.

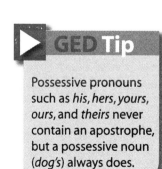

GED Tip

Possessive pronouns such as *his, hers, yours, ours,* and *theirs* never contain an apostrophe, but a possessive noun (*dog's*) always does.

Check your answers on page 164.

When you want to show exactly what someone said, you use quotation marks. Quotation marks tell the reader that you are giving someone's exact words.

Examples:

- The candidate promised, "I will never raise taxes."
- "I will never raise taxes," promised the candidate.

quotation
someone's exact words

A **quotation** usually begins with a capital letter. The punctuation mark at the end of the quotation always comes before the quotation mark.

When you write a question or an exclamation in quotation marks, include a question mark or an exclamation point. This punctuation should be placed before the last set of quotation marks.

Examples:

- She asked, "Why do you want to know?"
- "I love my new camera!" Jack said.

When you are quoting a statement, use a comma to set off the quotation from who said it.

Examples:

- "This is important," Marvin said.
- Marvin said, "This is important."
- "This," Marvin said, "is important."

When you write about people's statements but don't use their exact words, do not use quotation marks.

A politician is often quoted.

Examples:

- The candidate promised not to raise taxes.
- Jack said that he loves his new camera.
- I asked him where he was going after work.
- My friend said that Barack Obama is doing a fine job in Congress.

Add quotation marks to the sentences.

1. Let's go to the Brooklyn Museum, said Maria.

2. Is that near the aquarium? Bruce asked.

3. No, it is next to the Botanical Garden, Maria explained.

4. Oh! Bruce replied. I know where that is.

5. You could all come to my house afterwards, suggested my friend.

6. Say, that's a great idea! exclaimed Tina.

Add apostrophes where they are needed.

7. An explorers life is full of adventures and surprises.

8. Vasco da Gamas ships sailed to India.

9. Jacques Cartier explored Canadas coast.

10. Ponce de Leons adventures included searching for a fountain of youth.

11. Ferdinand Magellan crossed the worlds oceans.

12. Marco Polo explored Asias great land.

Write the contractions for the underlined words.

13. It is 10 o'clock. _____

14. The alarm clock did not ring. _____

15. The alarm was not set correctly. _____

16. I will be late! _____

17. I do not want to miss my bus! _____

Check your answers on page 164.

Words That Sound Alike

Some common words sound alike or almost alike. However, they have different spellings and different meanings. Often, it's hard to know when to use which word. Read the chart of words below.

who's	whose
it's	its
we're	were
they're	their, there
you're	your

The words written with apostrophes are contractions. Contractions are shortened versions of two words. Read the examples below, and notice the two words that form each contraction.

Examples: Contractions

- Who's in charge of this table? (Who is)
- It's my job. (It is)
- We're all together. (We are)
- They're our guests. (They are)
- You're a large group. (You are)

possessive pronoun
a pronoun that shows that something belongs to someone

The words without apostrophes in the chart are not contractions. For example, *its*, *their*, and *your* are **possessive pronouns**. *There* is an adverb meaning "in that place." For example: The photo is there.

Read the following sentences that use these possessive pronouns correctly.

Examples: Possessive Pronouns

- Whose sweater is this?
- Its buttons are loose.
- Where were you?
- Their tickets are there on the shelf.
- Was this your idea?

How do you know whether to use a contraction or a possessive pronoun in a sentence? There's a simple rule: Use the contraction only if you can replace it with two words.

"Who's in charge of this table?" can be changed to "Who is in charge of this table?" So, you know *who's* is correct. However, "Whose sweater is this?" cannot be changed to "Who is sweater is this?" This time you know you can't use *who's*. The correct word is *whose*.

Underline the correct form of the word in parentheses to complete each sentence. Remember to use a contraction only if you can replace the word with two words.

1. (Who's / Whose) going to take the bus to work?

2. Lenny tells me (you're / your) fixing the chimney today.

3. When did (your / you're) chimney start to crumble?

4. (It's / Its) time to put new mortar between the bricks.

5. The worst damage was done to (they're / their) car.

6. (Your / You're) going to need some help.

Underline the word or words that correctly complete each sentence.

7. (We're / Were) ready to go.

8. (We're / Were) you planning to come with us?

9. (Who's / Whose) keys are these?

10. (It's / Its) time for the dog to eat (it's / its) dinner.

11. (They're / Their) starting (their / they're) jobs today.

12. (It's / Its) time to do (you're / your) laundry.

13. (They're / Their) new car has a dent in (it's / its) fender.

14. If (you're / your) going to work overtime (you're / your) going to be paid more.

Check your answers on page 165.

Words that sound alike but have different meanings and different spellings are called **homonyms**. The chart below contains some common homonyms.

hour—60 minutes our—belonging to us	be—to exist bee—an insect
meet—to come together meat—flesh	know—to understand no—the opposite of *yes*
piece—a part peace—the opposite of war	pane—the glass in a window pain—hurt
red—a color read—the past tense of *read*	sea—a body of water see—to look
right—correct; the opposite of left; a privilege write—to put on paper	to—"I want to help." too—also two—the number 2
sail—to travel by boat sale—a bargain	through—"Go through the door." threw—the past tense of *throw*
weight—the amount something weighs wait—to pass time	sew—to stitch so—therefore
	weigh—to measure weight way—a manner: a direction
whole—entire hole—an opening	would—"Would you come with me?" wood—a material from trees

Underline the word or words that correctly complete each sentence.

1. We can't (sea / see) the (sea / see) from here.

2. Do you (know / no) the (way / weigh) to Yoshi's house?

3. Flora (rights / writes) very well.

4. (Hour / Our) train leaves in an (hour / our).

5. Have you (red / read) the directions?

6. Peg wants (two / to) go, (to / too).

Check your answers on page 165.

Practice

Underline the word that correctly completes each sentence.

1. (We're / Were) looking for a new mechanic.

2. (You're / Your) a very experienced electrician.

3. I think (it's / its) a good job.

4. (They're / There) planning to meet us later.

5. Put the boxes over (their / there).

6. (Whose / Who's) going to be there?

7. (Whose / Who's) car is that green one?

8. May I borrow (you're / your) lawn mower?

9. (Their / There) daughter goes to day care in the morning.

Replace the underlined word in each sentence with the correct homonym.

10. The answer is <u>know</u>. _____

11. Please <u>bee</u> ready tomorrow. _____

12. I stubbed my toe and am in <u>pane</u>. _____

13. The U.S. flag is <u>read</u>, white, and blue. _____

14. Did you eat the <u>hole</u> sandwich? _____

15. A bicycle has <u>too</u> wheels. _____

16. He can't <u>sea</u> without his glasses. _____

17. Martin Luther King, Jr., led the civil <u>writes</u> movement in the United States. _____

18. I'd like some <u>piece</u> and quiet. _____

19. The doctor checked my <u>wait</u>. _____

20. I went <u>two</u> the clinic after work. _____

Check your answers on page 165.

Learning a few spelling rules can help you spell many words correctly. The "*i* before *e*" rhyme is one helpful rule.

> *I* before *e*,
> except after *c*
> and when sounded as *a*,
> as in *neighbor* and *weigh*.

Read some familiar words that follow the rule of "*i* before *e*." Notice the placement of the *i* and *e*.

- piece   pie   friend

When *i* and *e* follow the letter *c*, the *e* comes first. Read these words and notice the *i* and *e*.

- receive   receipt   deceive

The *e* also comes before the *i* when the letters have the *a* sound. Read these words and notice the *i* and *e*.

- freight   sleigh   weight

Here are some exceptions to the "*i* before *e*" rule. You might want to memorize the spelling of these words.

either	height	ancient
neither	leisure	species
foreign	seize	science
forfeit	weird	conscience

Circle the misspelled word in each sentence. Write each word correctly.

1. She gave her freind a piece of pie. _____

2. You can't return that dress without a sales reciept.

_____

3. List your hieght and weight on the application form.

_____

Check your answers on page 165.

Here are some rules for spelling words when you add endings to the words. These rules apply to endings that start with a vowel, such as *-ing*, *-ed*, *-er*, and *-est*.

Rule 1: For most words, just add the ending.

- start + -ed = started
- feel + -ing = feeling
- remind + -er = reminder

Rule 2: If a word ends in *e*, drop the *e* and then add the ending.

- hope + -ing = hoping

Rule 3: If a one-syllable word ends in a consonant with a vowel before it, double the last letter and add the ending.

- hop + -ing = hopping
- fit + -ed = fitted
- fat + -er = fatter
- flat + -est = flattest

Rule 3 also applies to longer words that have the **accent** on the last **syllable** of the word.

- admit + -ed = admitted
- begin + -ing = beginning

All spelling rules have exceptions. If you want to know how to spell a word, try looking up different ways you think the word may be spelled in a dictionary.

accent
the stress you put on one part of a word when you say it

syllable
one or more letters in a word that make up a separate sound, for example, syl-la-ble

Add the endings *-ed* and *-ing* to these words. Follow the rules above.

1. work _____ _____

2. live _____ _____

3. plan _____ _____

4. talk _____ _____

5. remind _____ _____

Check your answers on page 165.

▶ GED Tip

Make flash cards of the words you misspell most often. Many times, the only way to learn correct spelling is to memorize.

Underline the word that correctly completes each sentence.

1. TV watching increases as people have more (leisure / liesure) time.

2. Some tools from (anceint / ancient) times were found in Africa.

3. Medical (sceince / science) continues to make progress.

4. Hazel is studying two (foreign / foriegn) languages.

5. (Neither / Niether) of us has been out sick all winter.

6. Did you (recieve / receive) the letter I sent you?

Add -*er* and -*est* to these words. Use the rules on page 105.

7. loud _____ _____

8. thin _____ _____

9. kind _____ _____

10. mad _____ _____

11. fine _____ _____

12. soft _____ _____

Add -*ed* and -*ing* to these words. Use the rules on page 105.

13. stop _____ _____

14. love _____ _____

15. control _____ _____

16. refer _____ _____

17. stress _____ _____

18. rule _____ _____

19. shop _____ _____

20. fix _____ _____

Rewrite each word below using the correct spelling.

21. prefered _____

22. neice _____

23. hieght _____

24. skateing _____

25. rememberring _____

26. youngr _____

27. permited _____

28. releif _____

Read this advertisement and circle the spelling mistakes. Then rewrite the ad correctly on the lines below.

If you are haveing computer trouble, CompWiz can help. We are experts in repairing any problem for any computer we recieve in our shop. Does your computer seem slow and slugish? Let us help you get rid of unneedded files. We are commited to our customers, and we guarantee satisfaction. You come as a customer, and you leave as a freind.

_____

_____

_____

_____

_____

_____

_____

Check your answers on page 165.

Knowing Where to Punctuate

Every sentence ends with a punctuation mark. Use a period, exclamation point, or question mark to show the end of a sentence. Use a comma when there is a small pause between words in a sentence.

 Strategy Listen for stops and pauses. Follow these steps.

1. Read your writing out loud.

2. Listen for stops. Stops are places where you use end punctuation.

3. Listen for pauses. Pauses are places where you may want to add a comma.

Exercise 1: Read this ad. Add end punctuation.

Good morning, dieters
Are you tired of eating the same old breakfast
Do you want a change
Are you worried about fat and calories
Then try our new low-calorie, high-fiber carrot muffin

Exercise 2: Read the rest of the ad. Add end punctuation. Add commas where you hear pauses. Then write your own sentence to end the ad.

It's a delicious new breakfast treat It has no sugar fat or

preservatives It's packed with fiber and real carrots You'll love it

_____

_____

_____

_____

Exercise 3: Rewrite the sentences, using correct punctuation.

The pyramids which are huge stone structures were built 5,000 years ago in Egypt. Scientists still wonder how they were built?

_____

_____

_____

Exercise 4: Each sentence in the paragraph below has a punctuation error. Rewrite the paragraph, using correct punctuation.

Who built the pyramids. Thousands of Egyptian slaves who were forced to work for the pharaoh labored for hundreds of years. They had no modern tools? How did they lift those gigantic blocks! Scientists think that they used levers pulleys and block-and-tackle. We may never know for sure and we will always try to discover more.

_____

_____

_____

_____

_____

_____

_____

Check your answers on page 166.

Previewing Test Questions

On the GED Writing Test, you find sets of questions based on paragraphs or passages. Each question asks you to correct a different error in the passage. One strategy for passing the GED Writing Test is to preview the test questions before you read the passage. This will give you an idea of what and where the errors may be.

 Strategy Try this strategy with the following example. Use these steps.

Step 1 Quickly skim the questions that go with the paragraph.

Step 2 Look through the answer choices. Find the correction that makes the most sense. Keep this correction in mind.

Step 3 Now read the paragraph. Pay special attention to the sentences mentioned in the questions.

Step 4 Read each question carefully and choose the correct answer.

Example

(1) Historians ask military men and women to save the letters and e-mails that they recieve when they are on active duty. (2) They also ask families to save letters sent home. (3) The stories contained in those letters will become an important part of history.

Which correction should be made to sentence 1?

(1) change <u>women</u> to <u>womans</u>

(2) change <u>letters</u> to <u>letteres</u>

(3) change <u>recieve</u> to <u>receive</u>

(4) no correction is necessary

In Step 1 you skimmed the question. In Step 2 you found the correction that made sense. In Step 3 you read the paragraph, paying special attention to Sentence 1. In Step 4 you answered the question. Choice (3) is correct. The *e* should come before the *i* in *receive*.

Practice the strategy. Use the steps that you learned. Circle the number of the correct answer.

(1) Historians ask military men and women to save the letters and e-mails that they receive when they are on active duty. (2) They also ask families to save letters sent from soldier's. (3) The stories in these letters will become an important part of hour history. (4) Organizations in the united states are collecting copies of soldiers' letters. (5) They will preserve the letters in books and Libraries.

1. Which correction should be made to sentence 2?

   (1) change They to Them
   (2) change families to familys
   (3) change letters to letter's
   (4) change soldier's to soldiers

2. Which correction should be made to sentence 3?

   (1) change stories to Stories
   (2) insert a comma after letters
   (3) change hour to our
   (4) no correction is necessary

3. Which correction should be made to sentence 4?

   (1) change Organizations to Organization's
   (2) change united states to United States
   (3) change copies to copys
   (4) change soldiers' to soldier's

4. Which correction should be made to sentence 5?

   (1) change will preserve to preserved
   (2) insert a comma after letters
   (3) change books to book's
   (4) change Libraries to libraries

Check your answers on page 166.

Read each paragraph and question carefully. Circle the number of the correct answer.

Questions 1–4 are based on the following paragraph.

(1) If you plan Weeks ahead of your moving date, you can avoid problems. (2) First, collect the write supplies. (3) You will need boxes tape, and newspaper or packing paper. (4) Next, borrow a handcart or wagon. (5) Finally, enlist the help of your freinds.

1. Which correction should be made to sentence 1?

(1) change you to You
(2) change Weeks to weeks
(3) insert a comma after of
(4) change problems to problem's

2. Which correction should be made to sentence 2?

(1) change First to first
(2) remove the comma after First
(3) change write to right
(4) no correction is necessary

3. Which correction should be made to sentence 3?

(1) insert a comma after need
(2) insert a comma after boxes
(3) change newspaper to Newspaper
(4) change the period to a question mark

4. Which correction should be made to sentence 5?

(1) remove the comma after Finally
(2) insert a comma after help
(3) change your to you're
(4) change freinds to friends

Questions 5–8 are based on the following paragraph.

(1) Please join me in welcoming our new copy room attendant Angela Delgado. (2) Ms. delgado will perform two roles in her job. (3) She will make all copies for the department, and she will keep track of all paper supplies for the office? (4) Ms. Delgado will report to work on june 1.

5. Which correction should be made to sentence 1?

   (1) change in to inn
   (2) change new to knew
   (3) insert a comma after attendant
   (4) change Angela Delgado to angela Delgado

6. Which correction should be made to sentence 2?

   (1) change delgado to Delgado
   (2) change Ms. to ms.
   (3) change two to too
   (4) change roles to role's

7. Which correction should be made to sentence 3?

   (1) add a comma after make
   (2) change the question mark to a period
   (3) remove the comma after department
   (4) no correction is necessary

8. Which correction should be made to sentence 4?

   (1) change will to Will
   (2) insert a comma after work
   (3) change june to June
   (4) no correction is necessary

Question 9 is based on the following paragraph.

(1) We have completed our year-end inventory, and its time to celebrate! (2) We hope you can join us Friday after work to enjoy an evening of thanks and appreciation.

9. Which correction should be made to sentence 1?

(1) insert a comma after <u>have</u>

(2) remove the comma after <u>inventory</u>

(3) change <u>its</u> to <u>it's</u>

(4) change <u>celebrate!</u> to <u>celebrate?</u>

Check your answers on page 166.

Unit 3 Skill Check-Up Chart

Check your answers. In the first column, circle the numbers of any questions that you missed. Then look across the rows to see the skills you need to review and the pages where you can find each skill.

Question	Skill	Page
1	Capitalizing in Sentences	78–81
8	Capitalizing Days and Dates	82–83
6	Capitalizing Names	84–87
7	Punctuating Sentence Endings	90–91
3, 5	Using Commas	92–95
9	Using Apostrophes	96–99
2	Words That Sound Alike	100–103
4	Spelling Rules	104-107

Unit 4   Writing Skills

In this unit you will learn about

- types of daily writing
- writing paragraphs
- the writing process
- narrative and descriptive writing
- explanatory and persuasive writing

topic sentence

edit

purpose

draft

You probably write something every day. Daily writing can include making a grocery list or filling out a form. You might also write a note to your child's teacher or a letter to a friend.

List one type of writing that you do during your day.

_____

_____

What type of writing would you like to improve?

_____

_____

paragraph
a group of sentences about one main idea

indented
moved in a few spaces

topic sentence
the sentence that tells what the rest of the paragraph is about

main idea
the most important idea in a paragraph

A **paragraph** is a group of sentences that relate to the same idea. The first line of a paragraph is **indented**, or moved in a few spaces, to show that the paragraph is beginning.

Every paragraph is about one idea. Many paragraphs have a topic sentence. A **topic sentence** tells the main point, or idea, of the paragraph. The other sentences in the paragraph give details that support, or help explain, the **main idea**.

Examples: Paragraph

<u>The best time to shop for groceries at the local Fresh-Mart is Tuesday mornings.</u> Fresh-Mart coupons are published in the Tuesday morning paper. In addition, Fresh-Mart offers Tuesday specials from 8 a.m. until noon. The store gets new produce on Monday nights, so the fruits and vegetables are always garden-fresh on Tuesday mornings.

In the example above, the topic sentence is underlined. All of the other sentences give details that support the main idea in the topic sentence of the paragraph.

When you write a paragraph, make sure that your topic sentence states the main idea. Make sure that the other sentences give details to help explain the main idea. A group of sentences that is not focused on one idea is not a paragraph. Read the example below.

Examples: Not a Paragraph

Car racing is fast becoming the most popular sport in America. My brother owns a very fast car. Automobiles have gotten very expensive. I was in a car accident last year.

Although this group of sentences looks like a paragraph, it is not. The sentences do not all support one main idea.

Write *P* if the group of sentences is a paragraph. Write *NP* if the group is not a paragraph.

1. _____ Paying bills is easy if you use a good system. First of all, collect the bills in one place, and pay them all on the same day. In this way, bills will be paid on time in a routine way. Set aside those bills you have questions about. Be sure to make the necessary phone calls that same day so that you do not forget.

2. _____ Miriam's son has been a great help to the family. When Miriam was sick, he took her to her doctor's appointments. He took care of the cats and cleaned her apartment. He also made sure that his father had three meals a day.

3. _____ The day of the neighborhood picnic was perfect. Last Tuesday it rained. My husband's company picnic is usually fun. Potato salad is a good picnic food.

4. _____ The rents at 401 Fairfax Street are too high. My mother pays less for her one-bedroom apartment. Please pay your rent on the first of the month. Fairfax Street is a very busy street. My children go to daycare in the Fairfax area.

Add two sentences to support each topic sentence. Be sure your sentences support the main idea.

5. Money is important, but it does not make life perfect.

_____

_____

6. The weekend weather was terrible.

_____

_____

GED **Tip**

On the GED Writing Test, you will write an essay. Use paragraphs to organize your ideas.

Check your answers on page 167.

Lesson 24 — Steps in the Writing Process

topic
the subject you write about

purpose
your reason for writing

Writing something other than a list takes time and planning. Good writers don't just sit down and quickly produce a perfect paragraph or letter. They use these steps:

> 1. Plan before you write.
> 2. Write a first draft.
> 3. Correct and edit.
> 4. Write the final version.

Step 1: Plan Before You Write

First, choose a **topic**. Write about something that interests you or about something you know a lot about. Your topic might be sports, a hobby, children, your work, or a past event.

Next, decide on your **purpose**, or reason for writing. For example, if your topic is exercise, your purpose could be to explain why you started exercising or to convince others to exercise.

Finally, make some notes about the facts your paragraph will contain.

Here is a plan for writing a paragraph about exercise.

Topic: Exercise

Purpose: To explain how and why I started exercising

What I will say: Why I started exercising; what I did; how I lost weight

In this lesson, you will plan and write a paragraph. First, you will need to make a plan. Choose your topic and purpose. Then list a few notes about what you will say about the topic.

Topic: _____

Purpose: _____

What I will say: _____

_____

Step 2: Write the First Draft

A **draft** is the first version of your paragraph. Here you put your ideas on paper without worrying about using correct spelling, punctuation, or grammar. You can correct these later.

draft
an early version of a paragraph or passage

The draft of your paragraph should have a topic sentence that tells the main idea, or what your paragraph is about.

1. Read this first draft of a paragraph about exercise. Underline the topic sentence.

My new years resilution was to become more activ. So when the store I work at offer us half-price memberships to the gym across the street, I joined. I choose to ride the exercise bicicle then I worked out on the machines. After a month, I lost four pounds. I have more energy and feel stronger. If I can do it, you can do it, too.

2. Write your first draft using the plan you made for your paragraph. Underline your topic sentence.

_____

_____

_____

_____

_____

_____

_____

_____

_____

Step 3: Correct and Edit Your Writing

edit
to correct mistakes in a
piece of writing

Once you have finished your first draft, it is time to **edit** it. Read your draft carefully, looking for mistakes. Use this checklist.

Editing Checklist

■ Is there a topic sentence that states the main idea?
If not, rewrite with a clear topic sentence.

■ Do all other sentences support the topic sentence?
If not, cross out unrelated sentences. Add one or more sentences that relate to the main idea.

■ Do the sentences sound correct when you read them?
If not, check your grammar. Check that each sentence is correct as written.

■ Are all words spelled correctly?
Use the dictionary to check words you are not sure of.

■ Is the punctuation and capitalization correct?
If not, correct it as needed.

Here is how the writer revised the paragraph about exercise.

My ~~new years resilution~~ was to became more ~~activ~~. So when the *(New Year's resolution)* *(active)*
store I work at ~~offer~~ us half-price memberships to the gym across the *(offered)*
street, I joined. I ~~choose~~ to ride the exercise ~~bicicle then~~ I worked out on *(chose)* *(bicycle. Then)*
the machines. After a month, I lost four pounds. I have more energy and
feel stronger. If I can do it, you can do it, too.

Notice that the writer corrected the spelling of many words. Also, punctuation was changed or added. Careful editing can change a rough draft into a clear paragraph.

Go back to your first draft on page 121 and edit it. Use the editing checklist above.

Step 4: Write the Final Version

Writing the final version of your paragraph is the next step. Rewrite or retype your draft, including all the corrections you made when you edited. Then read your paragraph one more time to make sure you fixed all your mistakes.

Read the final version of the paragraph about exercise.

My New Year's resolution was to become more active. So when the store I work at offered us half-price memberships to the gym across the street, I joined. I chose to ride the exercise bicycle. Then I worked out on the machines. After a month, I lost four pounds. I have more energy and feel stronger. If I can do it, you can do it, too.

Write the final version of your paragraph.

_____

_____

_____

_____

_____

_____

_____

_____

_____

_____

_____

_____

_____

> **GED Tip**
>
> You will not have the time or space to completely rewrite your essay on the GED Writing Test. Just be sure that your corrections are neat and readable.

Check your answer on page 167.

narrative
writing that tells about
an event

A **narrative** is a story about something that happened. It can be something that happened to you, someone you know, or someone you only know about. The event might have happened in your neighborhood or in another part of the world.

A narrative answers the five W questions: *who? what? when? where?* and *why?* The following narrative tells about an accident. The five W's are marked.

WHO ——→   Bobby Thomas, three-time winner of the amateur Junior Grand Prix auto race, once again avoided serious injury during a time trial.

WHEN ——→   The accident took place last Thursday evening at about 6:30 p.m. It was the first day of

WHERE ——→   qualifying at the Indianapolis Motor Speedway.

Thomas lost control of his car as he entered the first turn. Luckily, the car slammed

WHAT ——→   into the safety barrier. This barrier protects cars and drivers from more serious harm.

WHY ——→   Thomas said tire failure was the cause of the crash. Thomas was taken to the hospital by

WHEN ——→   ambulance. After a few hours he was released. His family stated that he was in good condition. He expects to be back at the track as

WHEN ——→   early as next week.

Cars in an auto race

Write a narrative paragraph. Be sure that your narrative answers the five W questions: *who? what? when? where?* **and** *why?*

Use one of these topics or make up a topic of your own.

- an exciting moment in your life
- a trip you have taken
- a storm or disaster that has happened in your area
- an act of kindness that you or someone else has done

_____

_____

_____

_____

_____

_____

_____

_____

The Writing Process

1. Plan before you write.
2. Write a first draft.
3. Correct and edit.
4. Write the final version.

Now read your first draft above carefully. Then edit it. Use the editing checklist on page 122. Write the final version of your paragraph below.

_____

_____

_____

_____

_____

GED Tip

You may need to use narrative writing when you write your GED Essay. Make sure your narrative writing is short, simple, and easy to follow.

_____

_____

_____

_____

Check your answers on page 168.

adjective
a word that describes a noun or pronoun by telling *which one, what kind,* or *how many*

A descriptive paragraph often describes a person, place, thing, or experience. It uses **adjectives** to make the writing come alive for the reader.

Read the following description of a place. Then underline each adjective.

I grew up in a small town in Kansas. It was mostly farmland, with green fields extending in all directions. Our neighbors grew tall yellow corn, large red tomatoes, and juicy green lettuce. Some farmers raised brown, black, and white cows. In the evenings we could hear the cows mooing. At night the air was cool and crisp. There were millions of bright stars in the dark black sky.

A farm in Kansas

Read the following description of an animal.

My dog Ranger is a mutt. I got him when he was a tiny puppy. He has long brown hair, floppy ears, and a little tail that he wags all the time. He runs fast to chase a stick and jumps high to catch a ball. His loud bark warns me that someone is at the door. Ranger is my best friend.

Reread the above paragraph about Ranger. Underline each adjective. Above each underlined word, write a different adjective that might be used there.

Check your answers on page 168.

Write a descriptive paragraph about someone you know. The person can be a friend, a parent, your husband or wife, your child, or anyone else. Use adjectives and pronouns in your description.

_____

_____

_____

_____

_____

_____

_____

_____

Be sure each paragraph

- is indented
- has a topic sentence
- has other sentences that support the main idea

Write a descriptive paragraph about a place or an object. For example, you might describe a favorite room in your home or a special photograph.

_____

_____

_____

_____

_____

_____

_____

_____

_____

▶ **GED Tip**

Using adjectives in your writing can help the reader "see" what you mean. This will help improve your GED Essay.

Check your answers on page 168.

transition words
words such as *first, next,* and *then* that link one step to the next

An explanatory paragraph tells how to do something. The steps you use are organized in time order from first to last. Use **transition words** to make the steps clear.

Examples of Transition Words

- first
- second
- now
- next
- then
- before
- after
- finally

Here is an explanatory paragraph that gives directions to someone's house. The transition words are underlined.

To get to my house, take the subway to Park Street. When you get outside, <u>first</u> walk two blocks straight ahead to Market Street. <u>Then</u> turn left. <u>After</u> you pass the Chinese restaurant, you'll see a house with a yellow door. My apartment is number 6. <u>Before</u> you come up, ring the bell.

Read the following paragraph explaining how to do a push-up. Underline the transition words.

To do a push-up, first lie face down on the floor. Second, flex your feet so your toes are on the floor and your heels are sticking up. Next, put your palms on the floor beside your shoulders. Then, straighten your arms and push yourself up, keeping your back straight. Finally, bend your arms and lower your body. Don't collapse! Repeat.

Check your answers on page 168.

Write an explanatory paragraph. Explain how to do something or how to get somewhere. Use transition words.

Use one of these topics or make up a topic of your own.

- how to swing a bat or shoot a basket
- how to diaper a baby
- how to get to your home from a bus stop or highway exit
- how to cook your favorite food

_____

_____

_____

_____

_____

_____

_____

_____

_____

The Writing Process

1. Plan before you write.
2. Write a first draft.
3. Correct and edit.
4. Write the final version.

Now read your first draft above carefully. Then edit it. Use the editing checklist on page 122. Write the final version of your paragraph below.

_____

_____

_____

_____

_____

_____

_____

_____

_____

 **GED Tip**

On the GED Essay, keep your explanations short and simple. Long and wordy explanations can be confusing.

Check your answers on page 168.

Writing a Topic Sentence

Writing strong topic sentences will help you to be a good writer. A good topic sentence states your main idea. It tells the reader what the paragraph will be about. It is a general statement that ties together all of the ideas in the paragraph.

 Strategy Write a strong topic sentence. Follow these steps.

1. Choose the main point you want to make about a topic.

2. List some details that support this main point.

3. Write a complete sentence stating the main idea. The sentence should cover all of the ideas on your list.

Exercise 1: Read each topic. Think of the main point you want to make about each topic. List some details to support the main point. Finally, write a topic sentence that states the main idea.

1.   traveling by train

main point: <u>I like traveling by train</u>

details: <u>convenient, relaxing, no traffic or parking worries</u>

topic sentence: <u>Traveling by train is comfortable and convenient.</u>

2.   applying for a job

main point: _____

details: _____

topic sentence: _____

3.   your best friend

main point: _____

details: _____

topic sentence: _____

A good paragraph includes only details that support the main idea in your topic sentence. Edit your writing to remove any details that are not about the main idea.

 Strategy Be sure your topic sentence ties together all ideas in the paragraph. Follow these steps.

1. Read your completed paragraph.
2. Check that each sentence supports the topic sentence.
3. Cross out sentences that do not support the topic sentence.

Exercise 2: Carefully read each paragraph. Cross out the sentence that does not support the topic sentence of the paragraph.

1. In the Midwest, each season has its own personality. Spring brings beautiful flowers and lots of green. Summer is a time of sun and warmth. The season of fall is full of brisk wind and bright leaves. I once took a vacation in the fall. Finally, winter brings snow and ice.

2. Our house has been in poor condition for some time. The upstairs sink is leaking. My cousin wants to be a plumber. The basement was supposed to be painted last year, but it never was done. We are waiting for a locksmith to fix the front lock.

Exercise 3: Write a topic sentence for each paragraph.

1. _____

   Mary has never been late in her three years of working here. She is respected by her coworkers. She has gladly taken on many difficult projects. She is an excellent listener and problem solver.

2. _____

   A childcare worker must be very patient. He or she must truly enjoy being with children. A childcare worker needs to be dependable, and above all, he or she needs a great sense of humor.

Check your answers on page 169.

Responding to a Writing Topic

On the GED Writing Test, Part 2, you will be given a topic to write an essay about. There is no right or wrong response to the topic. Your writing will be judged on how well you have responded to the topic and how clear your writing is.

To respond to a topic, first make a list of your ideas. Then write a good topic sentence that sums up your ideas. Finally, use your ideas to write sentences that support the main idea.

 Strategy Try this strategy with the following example. Use these steps.

Step 1 Read the topic carefully.

Step 2 List your ideas about the topic.

Step 3 Summarize your ideas in a topic sentence.

Step 4 Use your ideas to write the rest of the paragraph.

Example

TOPIC

Many people think it is okay to lie in order to protect another person's feelings. Do you think lying is ever okay? Write a paragraph that states your opinion. Use details to support your point of view.

Lying is never a good idea, even if you are trying to protect someone's feelings. Most people would want to know the truth even if it was difficult to hear. For example, telling your friend she looks good in pink when you really think it looks awful on her doesn't help your friend. It is better to be honest and help her find something that improves her appearance.

In Step 1 the writer read the topic carefully. In Step 2 she thought about what she had to say on the topic and listed some ideas. In Step 3 she wrote a topic sentence that stated her main idea. In Step 4 she supported her opinion with other sentences.

Practice

Practice the strategy. Use the steps that you learned. Write a paragraph in response to each topic.

TOPIC A

"Living in the city is more difficult than living in the country." Do you agree or disagree with this statement? Write a paragraph that states your opinion. Use specific details to support your point of view.

_____

_____

_____

_____

_____

_____

_____

TOPIC B

What is your favorite time of year? Write a paragraph that describes your favorite season. Use specific details and examples.

_____

_____

_____

_____

_____

_____

_____

Check your answers on page 169.

Read each topic carefully. List your ideas, and then write a paragraph for each topic. When you have finished writing, go back to correct and edit your work.

TOPIC A

Think of something you are good at. In a paragraph, explain how to do this activity.

_____

_____

_____

_____

_____

_____

_____

_____

_____

_____

_____

_____

_____

_____

_____

_____

TOPIC B

In your opinion, who is the most important American alive today?

Write a paragraph to express your opinion. Give reasons and examples to support your point of view.

_____

_____

_____

_____

_____

_____

_____

_____

_____

_____

_____

_____

_____

_____

_____

_____

_____

_____

TOPIC C

What would a perfect day be like for you? Write a paragraph describing your perfect day. Use specific details.

_____

_____

_____

_____

_____

_____

_____

_____

_____

_____

_____

Check your answers on page 169.

Unit 4 Skill Check-Up Chart

After you have written your essays, correct them using the editing checklist on page 122. Then look at the chart below to see what type of essay each topic required and the pages where you can practice each essay type.

Topic	Essay Style	Pages
A	Explanatory	128–129
B	Persuasive	130–131
C	Descriptive	126–127

Writing Posttest

This *Writing Posttest* will give you an idea of how well you have learned the writing skills in this book.

You will read paragraphs and answer questions. Choose the number of the correct answer. You will also write a paragraph about a topic that you are given.

There is no time limit.

Questions 1–4 are based on the following paragraph.

(1) Do you remember what it were like to be a kid in the summer? (2) It seemed there was nothing to do but eat ice cream, play with friends, and daydream you're day away. (3) The routines of school and homework were sudden gone. (4) As we get older, it seems weve got more responsibilities and less time for fun activities.

1. Which correction should be made to sentence 1?

    (1) change Do to Does
    (2) change were to was
    (3) change be to being
    (4) no correction is necessary

2. Which correction should be made to sentence 2?

    (1) change seemed to seem
    (2) change was to were
    (3) change daydream to daydreaming
    (4) change you're to your

3. Which correction should be made to sentence 3?

    (1) change routines to routine's
    (2) change were to been
    (3) change sudden to suddenly
    (4) no correction is necessary

4. Which correction should be made to sentence 4?

    (1) change weve to we've
    (2) change got to get
    (3) change responsibilities to responsibilities'
    (4) change activities to activitys

Questions 5–8 are based on the following paragraph.

(1) Shoppers looking for regular bargains every day should try joining a warehouse club. (2) A member of a warehouse club is able to buy everything from bulk grocerys to tires and electronics. (3) Some shoppers do they're regular food shopping, but they shop only once a month. (4) Some shoppers taked advantage of huge discounts and buy DVD players and televisions.

5. Which correction should be made to sentence 1?

    (1) change Shoppers to Shopper's
    (2) change regular to regularly
    (3) change try to trying
    (4) no correction is necessary

6. Which correction should be made to sentence 2?

    (1) change is to was
    (2) change is to are
    (3) change grocerys to groceries
    (4) change electronics to electronices

7. Which correction should be made to sentence 3?

    (1) change shoppers to shoppers'
    (2) change they're to their
    (3) change shop to shopped
    (4) change month to monthly

8. Which correction should be made to sentence 4?

    (1) change taked to take
    (2) change taked to took
    (3) change advantage to advantige
    (4) change buy to buyed

Questions 9–12 are based on the following paragraph.

(1) As an employee of Wintech, you are responsible for reading the company handbook. (2) And signing the release forms. (3) Either Ms. Anderson or her assistants are available to answer any questions. (4) The handbook can help make you a smart, effective, and be a productive employee. (5) Please be sure you read it by Monday it is an important part of our training.

9. Which revision should be made to the underlined portion of sentences 1 and 2? If the original is the best way, choose option (1).

    (1) handbook. And signing
    (2) Handbook. And signing
    (3) handbook and signing
    (4) handbook, And signing

10. Which revision should be made to the underlined portion of sentence 3? If the original is the best way, choose option (1).

    (1) her assistants are available
    (2) her assistants is available
    (3) her assistant's is available
    (4) her assistants was available

11. Which revision should be made to the underlined portion of sentence 4? If the original is the best way, choose option (1).

    (1) effective, and be a productive
    (2) effectively, and be a productive
    (3) effective and be a productive
    (4) effective, and productive

12. Which revision should be made to the underlined portion of sentence 5? If the original is the best way, choose option (1).

    (1) Monday it is an important
    (2) Monday. It is an important
    (3) Monday it was an important
    (4) Monday, it is an important

Questions 13–16 are based on the following paragraph.

(1) Even a small porch or landing can make a great place for a Garden. (2) It is best to start in may and to use small clay or plastic pots with good potting soil. (3) Many plants are easy to grow and they just need a little sun and some water. (4) Some flowering plants may need deep containers to help their roots grow.

13. Which correction should be made to sentence 1?

    (1) change porch to Porch
    (2) change make to makes
    (3) insert a comma after landing
    (4) change Garden to garden

14. Which correction should be made to sentence 2?

    (1) change pots to pot's
    (2) change soil to Soil
    (3) change may to May
    (4) no correction is necessary

15. Which correction should be made to sentence 3?

    (1) change are to is
    (2) insert a comma after grow
    (3) change need to needs
    (4) no correction is necessary

16. Which correction should be made to sentence 4?

    (1) change Some to Sum
    (2) change containers to containeres
    (3) change their to there
    (4) no correction is necessary

Questions 17–20 are based on the following paragraph.

(1) The potluck dinner on Saturday night, was a big success. (2) My roommate's Mother cooked a huge roast and a ham. (3) Although Cindy did'nt come, most of our other neighbors were there. (4) We recieved many compliments on our new home.

17. Which correction should be made to sentence 1?

    (1) change dinner to Dinner

    (2) remove the comma after night

    (3) change success to sucess

    (4) no correction is necessary

18. Which correction should be made to sentence 2?

    (1) change roommate's to roommates

    (2) change Mother to mother

    (3) change cooked to cook

    (4) no correction is necessary

19. Which correction should be made to sentence 3?

    (1) change Cindy to cindy

    (2) change did'nt to didn't

    (3) remove the comma after come

    (4) change there to their

20. Which correction should be made to sentence 4?

    (1) change recieved to received

    (2) insert a comma after compliments

    (3) change our to hour

    (4) change home to Home

Writing a Paragraph

21. What is your favorite movie or TV show? Write a paragraph that describes it. Use specific details and examples.

When you are finished, check and edit your work. Watch out for spelling, punctuation, and grammar mistakes. Correct errors neatly on your paper.

_____

_____

_____

_____

_____

_____

_____

_____

_____

_____

_____

_____

_____

_____

_____

_____

_____

_____

When you finish the Writing Posttest, check your answers on page 169. Then look at the chart on page 146.

Skills Review Chart

This chart shows you which skills you should review. Check your answers. In the first column, circle the number of any questions you missed. Then look across the row to find out which skills you should review as well as the page numbers on which you find instruction on those skills. Compare the items you circled in the *Skills Review Chart* to those you circled in the *Skills Preview Chart* to see the progress you've made.

Questions	Skill	Pages
2, 6, 7	Nouns, Pronouns, and Adjectives	14–31
1, 8	Verbs and Adverbs	32–49
9, 10, 11, 12	Complete Sentences	58–69
13, 14, 18	Capitalization	78–89
4, 15, 17, 19	Punctuation	90–99
20	Spelling	100–107
21	Writing Paragraphs	116–131

No correction is necessary: 3, 5, 16

Glossary

accent the stress you put on one part of a word when you say it. *page 105*

adjective a word that describes a noun or pronoun by telling *which one, what kind,* or *how many. pages 28 and 126*

adverb a word that describes a verb, an adjective, or another adverb. *page 46*

antecedent the noun to which a pronoun refers. *page 25*

apostrophe a punctuation mark that can be used to show possession or ownership. *page 20*

base form the simple form of the verb without any endings. *page 32*

capitalize to write with a capital letter. *page 78*

compound object two or more objects, usually joined by *and* or *or. page 16*

compound subject two or more subjects, usually joined by *and* or *or. pages 16 and 64*

conjunction a connecting word such as *and, but, or,* and *so* used with a comma to connect two complete thoughts. *page 94*

consonant any letter of the alphabet that isn't a vowel. *page 17*

contraction two words joined together to form one word. *page 96*

draft an early version of a paragraph or passage. *page 121*

edit to correct mistakes in a piece of writing. *page 122*

emphasize to make important. *page 79*

exception something that doesn't follow a rule. *page 18*

future tense the forms of a verb that expresses future time. *page 32*

helping verb a verb like *have, be,* and *do* that is used with other verbs. *pages 33 and 62*

homonym a word that sounds like another word but has a different meaning and usually a different spelling. *page 102*

indented moved in a few spaces. *page 118*

independent clause a group of words that can stand alone as a sentence. *page 60*

irregular verb a verb that doesn't have the *-ed* ending in the past tense and past participle. *page 34*

main idea the most important idea in a paragraph. *page 118*

narrative writing that tells about an event. *page 124*

noun a word that names a person, place, thing, or idea. *page 12*

noun-pronoun agreement a noun and a pronoun that have the same number and gender (male or female or neutral). *page 26*

object a word that receives the action of the verb in a sentence. *page 14*

object pronoun a pronoun that replaces the object in a sentence. *page 24*

opinion a person's view about an issue; an opinion is based on personal judgment and not always on fact. *page 130*

paragraph a group of sentences about one main idea. *page 118*

parallel structure all words or phrases of a series in the same form. *page 68*

past tense the forms of a verb that express past time. *page 33*

pause to stop briefly. *page 92*

personal pronoun a pronoun that replaces either the subject noun or the object noun in a sentence. *page 24*

plural more than one. *page 17*

possession ownership or belonging. *page 20*

possessive pronoun a pronoun that shows that something belongs to someone. *pages 25 and 100*

predicate the words that tell what the subject is or does. The predicate includes the verb. *pages 12 and 58*

present tense the forms of a verb that express present time. *page 32*

pronoun a word that can replace a noun in a sentence. *page 24*

punctuation marks symbols used in writing to make the meaning of sentences clear. *page 90*

purpose your reason for writing. *page 120*

quotation someone's exact words. *page 98*

regular verb a verb that has the *-ed* ending in the past tense and past participle. *page 33*

relationship a connection that is often personal. *page 84*

return address the address a letter comes from. *page 86*

run-on sentence two or more complete thoughts that are written together without correct punctuation. *page 60*

sentence a group of words that contains a subject, a verb, and a complete thought. *pages 12 and 58*

sentence fragment a group of words that is not a sentence. *page 61*

series a group of three or more words or phrases joined by commas and *and* or *or*. *page 68*

set off to separate. *page 92*

singular only one. *page 17*

specific exact, definite. *page 78*

state to say in words. *page 90*

statement a sentence that gives information and facts. *page 90*

subject the person or thing that a sentence is about. *pages 12 and 58*

subject pronoun a pronoun that replaces the subject in a sentence. *page 24*

subject-verb agreement the subject and the verb must agree in number; if the subject is plural, the verb must be in the plural form. *page 42*

syllable one or more letters in a word that make up a separate sound, for example, syl-la-ble. *page 105*

tense the form of the verb that shows the time of its action. *page 32*

title a word used before a person's name, such as *Mrs.* or *Dr. page 84*

topic the subject you write about. *page 120*

topic sentence the sentence that tells what the rest of the paragraph is about. *page 118*

transition words words such as *first*, *next*, and *then* that link one step to the next. *page 128*

verb the word that shows action or a state of being. *page 12*

vowel one of these letters of the alphabet: *a, e, i, o, u. page 17*

Answers and Explanations

Page 4

1. I carried the (boxs) upstairs.
2. (Ladys) and gentlemen, please sit down.
3. Cut the sandwich into two (halfs).
4. My (childs) are old enough to go to school.
5. he 6. me 7. Her 8. We
9. They live in a big red brick house.
10. This long wool scarf is mine.
11. My new shoes are comfortable.

Page 5

12. Walter (try) to call you last night.
13. She (worked) at her day job next week.
14. They (working) late every day.
15. Nate and Vera (is) married.
16. Neither Nate's parents nor Vera's mother (live) nearby.
17. My children, but not my wife, (has) red hair.
18. Rosa speaks (soft).
19. Kim changed the tire (quick).
20. (Sudden), he jumped up.

Page 6

21.	C	26.	starts
22.	I	27.	am
23.	I	28.	watches
24.	I	29.	walk
25.	I	30.	have

Page 7

31. (the) bus stop is across Main Street.
32. My birthday is in (july).
33. My (Husband) drives a bus.

34. I made an appointment with (dr.) Shih.
35. When is (thanksgiving)?
36. Do I turn right or left at the corner ⊙
37. I borrowed (Marys) radio.
38. We bought bread, ham, and cheese ⊙at the store.
39. "I got a new job, said Manny.⁹⁹
40. It is time to stop⊙and clean up.

Page 8

41. Please (develope) this film.
42. The recipe says to (seperate) the eggs.
43. That man looks (familier).
44. Did you (recieve) a package from the warehouse?
45. Her grandmother's ring is (valuble).
46. I am (realy) too tired to go with you.
47. She (preferrs) chicken to fish.
48. Aldo is (fourty) years old.
49. He is (allready) a citizen.
50. The (calandar) on the wall has nice pictures.

Page 9

51. Paragraphs will vary. Share your paragraph with your teacher. Here is a sample paragraph.

    I would like to be a professional basketball player. I am over six feet tall, and I have been playing basketball since I was young. I almost never miss a shot and am a good team member. I love the game. Basketball players make a lot of money, and I wouldn't mind that either.

Unit 1 Lesson 1

Page 12

1. Greg
2. Bicycles
3. plays
4. is
5. smiled
6. yes
7. yes
8. no

Page 13

1. She 2. Alec 3. Fruit 4. You 5. Nora
6. Joan (is) Steven's friend.
7. Steven (teaches) kindergarten.
8. He (drives) his car to work.
9. The car (broke) down yesterday.
10. Joan (took) him to work.

There are many possible sentences. Here are some examples.

11. I would like to live in Mexico.
12. I like being close to the bus stop.
13. I really admire my brother Peter.

Lesson 2

Page 15

1. Doris read the (memo) .
2. Three people attended the (meeting).
3. Bob wrote a (report) .
4. The memo was four pages long.
5. The meeting lasted a long time.
6. Bob's report is a good one.

There are many possible sentences. Here are some examples:

7. The telephone rang.
   I bought a new telephone.
8. The water dripped from the faucet.
   Jennifer drank water.

9. The chair was pushed under the table.
   Mark sat in the chair.
10. Kate is our neighbor.
    We took Kate to the clinic.

Page 16

There are many possible sentences. Here are some examples:

   Kevin and Danny rented an apartment.

   I remember buying milk and eggs yesterday.

There are many possible proper nouns. Here are some examples:

1. Ella Fitzgerald
2. Main Street
3. Sally Maynard
4. Beach Grille

Page 17

1. apples
2. trucks
3. days
4. hats
5. dishes
6. inches
7. taxes
8. misses
9. cities
10. flies
11. babies
12. lilies

Page 18

1. wives
2. calves
3. wolves
4. shelves
5. feet
6. women
7. beliefs
8. deer

Page 19

1. Danita borrows (books) from the library every week.
2. The librarian sorts new (novels).
3. Her children like the (trips) to the library.
4. They read (books) about animals and sports.
5. The library has (magazines) too.
6. Many people borrow (CDs).
7. Mr. Garcia borrows (DVDs).
8. Libraries inspire (people) to learn.
9. Atlanta
10. Patty Griffin

There are many possible sentences. Here are some examples:

11. Denver and Chicago are beautiful cities.

12. We ate dinner and played games.

13. friends   **15.** keys   **17.** factories

14. men   **16.** watches   **18.** lives

Lesson 3

Page 20

1. woman's
2. worker's
3. car's
4. Dr. White's
5. bus's
6. radiator's
7. Silas's
8. Uncle Chris's
9. bird's
10. Mrs. Jones's
11. brother's
12. shop's

Page 21

1. benches'
2. cities'
3. Johnsons'
4. cats'
5. Smiths'
6. girls'
7. dog's
8. players

Page 22

1. women's
2. mice's
3. deer's
4. feet's
5. Lucas's
6. cook's
7. beaches'
8. grandchildren's
9. moose's
10. sheep's
11. people's
12. match's
13. wives'
14. girls'

Page 23

1. company's
2. activities
3. employees'
4. children's
12. mother's
13. calves'
14. city's
15. Mill's

5. Jones's
6. women's
7. boss's
8. Wall's
9. groups'
10. men's
11. Isabel's
16. people's
17. everyone's
18. Andreas's
19. plan's
20. mayor's
21. child's

Lesson 4

Page 24

1. They   **2.** it   **3.** She

Anna and I had a picnic in the park. We laid the blanket down. Unfortunately, we laid it on an ant bed. The ants weren't too happy with us . They crawled all over the blanket. Anna was supposed to bring popsicles, but she forgot them at home. Anna and I decided that next time, we would let someone else plan the picnic.

Page 25

1. Her   **3.** theirs   **5.** His

2. Their   **4.** its

Page 26

1. (Tyrone and I) decided to replace <u>our</u> dishwasher.
2. The (dishwasher) was old, and <u>it</u> leaked water onto the floor.
3. My (neighbor) said <u>she</u> found a good dishwasher at B&B Appliances.
4. The (salespeople) there know what <u>they</u> are doing.
5. After (Tyrone and I) purchased the dishwasher, <u>we</u> went next door.
6. The (shop) next door was new, and <u>it</u> had many interesting things.
7. The (owner) of the shop said <u>she</u> used to travel all over the world.
8. She had (rugs) from India, and <u>they</u> were beautiful.
9. (I) wanted to buy a purple rug, but <u>I</u> didn't see any.
10. (Tyrone) bought a decorated pot for <u>his</u> garden.

Page 27

1. I
2. We
3. me
4. them
5. Yours
6. He, her
7. This (work) is hard because <u>it</u> requires both brains and muscles.
8. The (bosses) ask a lot from <u>their</u> employees.
9. When (Arturo and John) asked for time off, <u>they</u> were denied.
10. Each (man) must be able to do <u>his</u> own measurements and calculations.
11. The (doctor) answered <u>her</u> phone.
12. When (Oscar) left, <u>he</u> took the car.
13. (Lily and Sam) hated <u>their</u> costumes.

14. Its
15. her
16. their
17. His
18. Our

Lesson 5

Page 28

You can describe the food in many ways. Here are some examples:

moist, flaky fish
creamy mashed potatoes
fresh string beans
crisp green salad
steamy, hot coffee
low-fat ice cream

Page 29

There are many adjectives you can use in sentences 1–7. Here are some examples:

1. Thanksgiving dinner was <u>delicious</u> and <u>hectic</u>.
2. Mom's clean house smelled <u>homey</u>.
3. The turkey was <u>moist</u> and <u>tasty</u>.
4. My <u>active</u> nephews were <u>loud</u>.
5. Mom's <u>crazy</u> dog barked loudly.
6. For dessert I had <u>homemade</u> apple pie.
7. At the end of the night, I felt <u>happy</u>.
8. this
9. these
10. Those
11. These
12. this

Page 30

1. One <u>important</u> job at Pro-Line is sorting the mail.
2. The <u>first</u> job on your list is to sort the mail.
3. The <u>important</u> mail must be delivered now.
4. All <u>cardboard</u> boxes must be recycled.

There are many sentences you can write for exercises 5–7. Here are some examples:

5. My happy dog loves to swim.

6. The runner came in second place.

7. My little sister has red hair.

Page 31

1. that
3. These
5. this, that

2. this
4. Those

There are many adjectives you can use in sentences 6–12. Here are some examples:

6. That man is <u>older</u>.

7. Her coat looks <u>ragged</u>.

8. My new pet is a <u>lazy</u> cat.

9. The weather is very <u>unpredictable</u>.

10. We went to see the <u>horror</u> movie.

11. The <u>anniversary</u> party lasted very late.

12. The firefighters were <u>exhausted</u>.

13. Stacey has a <u>small</u>, <u>tidy</u> desk.

14. The <u>new</u> neighbors seem <u>nice</u>.

15. <u>Those</u> <u>little</u> boys are brothers.

16. They have <u>brown</u> hair and <u>blue</u> eyes.

17. Puerto Rico has <u>many</u> <u>beautiful</u> <u>sandy</u> beaches.

18. It also contains a <u>tropical</u> rain forest.

19. In the rain forest are <u>rare</u> birds and <u>big</u>, <u>colorful</u> flowers.

20. The paper advertised for a <u>hardworking</u>, <u>experienced</u> printer.

Lesson 6

Page 33

1. Tom <u>seems</u> happy. Base form: seem

2. Sandy <u>passed</u> the mall on her way home. Base form: pass

3. She <u>has painted</u> only one wall so far. Base form: paint

4. <u>Are</u> they <u>looking</u> for an apartment? Base form: look

5. No, they <u>are waiting</u> until summer. Base form: wait

6. They <u>are saving</u> their money first. Base form: save

7. Jane and Alexander <u>clapped</u> their hands in joy. Base form: clap

8. Kelly <u>is listening</u> to her music. Base form: listen

9. He <u>has decided</u> not to go. Base form: decide

10. <u>Are</u> you <u>talking</u> to us? Base form: talk

Page 34

11. He <u>drove</u> to work. Base form: drive

12. It <u>began</u> to rain. Base form: begin

13. He <u>has written</u> the report. Base form: write

14. We <u>won</u> by two points! Base form: win

15. I <u>sent</u> the letter by airmail. Base form: send

16. They <u>met</u> at the bowling alley. Base form: meet

17. The sweater <u>felt</u> soft. Base form: feel

18. Aaron <u>thinks</u> highly of you. Base form: think

19. They <u>have become</u> best friends. Base form: become

20. Alice and Kim <u>had</u> a great time. Base form: have

Page 35

1. gone	**5.** caught	**9.** present
2. begun	**6.** past	**10.** future
3. known	**7.** past	**11.** past
4. taken	**8.** present	**12.** future

Page 36

1. hit	**8.** sweep	**15.** fell
2. prepare	**9.** began	**16.** struck
3. defeat	**10.** see	**17.** broken
4. injure	**11.** slept	**18.** said
5. lose	**12.** find	**19.** come
6. win	**13.** lost	**20.** taught
7. have	**14.** got	

Page 37

21. called	**25.** needed
22. wanted	**26.** recommended
23. was	**27.** will be
24. will have	

Maria and David <u>watched</u> a television program on Channel 5. The show <u>was</u> about race car drivers. The show's host <u>spoke</u> with several well-known drivers. The stories of these men and women <u>were</u> fascinating. Maria <u>said</u> she <u>hoped</u> to race cars professionally some day. David <u>was</u> more interested in fixing and maintaining race cars. David and Maria <u>talked</u> for hours about their plans for their future in car racing.

Page 38

1. working	**3.** written
2. written	**4.** worked

Page 39

1. I <u>may have</u> (seen) this movie before.

2. <u>Can</u> you (help) me?

3. Sam <u>might</u> (come) with us.

4. <u>Would</u> you (like) some coffee?

Page 40

1. Did you fix the leaky faucet?

2. Are you copying the reports?

3. Did Henry put new tires on the car?

4. Has he been trying to get a new job?

5. Have you met them before?

6. Has the judge arrived in his chambers?

7. Has Shelly told her mother the good news?

8. Will they leave for Miami tomorrow?

9. Should I wake the children now?

10. Can they sleep a little longer?

11. Charles <u>may be</u> (joining) the armed services.

12. He <u>has been</u> (thinking) about it for months.

13. Gerald, his father, <u>might</u> (object).

14. He <u>should</u> (let) Charles decide for himself.

Page 41

15. Charles's mother <u>must be</u> (worrying).

16. She <u>will be</u> (turning) seventy soon.

17. Did	**21.** will have	**25.** go
18. Are	**22.** did	**26.** been
19. will have	**23.** seen	**27.** be
20. will be	**24.** help	**28.** come

There are many possible sentences you could write. Here are some examples:

29. This dinner would be great if Joe could come.

30. He might arrive late.

31. We should hold dinner until he gets here.

32. He must be working late tonight.

Lesson 8

Page 42

1. signs	**5.** runs	**9.** like
2. go	**6.** watch	**10.** draws
3. plays	**7.** drives	**11.** helps
4. play	**8.** live	**12.** enjoy

Page 43

1. is	**4.** has	**7.** were
2. are	**5.** are	**8.** were
3. have	**6.** was	**9.** was

Page 44

1. teaches	**3.** catches	**5.** hurries
2. carries	**4.** walks	**6.** washes

Page 45

1. swims	**7.** have	**13.** fishes
2. arrive	**8.** is	**14.** dries
3. starts	**9.** were	**15.** buys
4. visit	**10.** Are	**16.** watches
5. am	**11.** has	**17.** hurries
6. is	**12.** kisses	**18.** worries

Lesson 9

Page 46

There are many adverbs you could add to sentences 1–3. Here are some examples:

1. fast	**2.** quickly	**3.** softly

Page 47

1. quickly	**4.** easily
2. smoothly	**5.** He speaks clearly.
3. loudly	**6.** She writes cleverly.

The order of sentences 7–9 may vary.

7. Loudly, they laughed at her jokes.

8. They laughed loudly at her jokes.

9. They loudly laughed at her jokes.

Page 48

1. Suddenly	**9.** badly
2. immediately	**10.** really
3. softly	**11.** carefully
4. completely	**12.** usually
5. patiently	**13.** easily
6. accurately	**14.** truly
7. carefully	**15.** gently
8. quickly	

The order of sentences 16–18 may vary.

16. Easily, I passed my driver's test.

17. I easily passed my driver's test.

18. I passed my driver's test easily.

Page 49

19. Sam and Nancy (woke) up early on Saturday morning.

20. Their alarm clock (buzzed) suddenly.

21. They were very (eager) to start the day.

22. Quickly, they (dressed) and got some coffee.

23. They usually (get) to the first yard sale by nine o'clock.

24. Sellers often (display) their best products in the morning.

25. The women carefully (look) through piles of clothes.

26. They rarely (end) their day without a purchase.

There are many adverbs you can add to sentences 27–32. Here are some examples:

27. Each day, airplanes fly <u>loudly</u> through the skies above.

28. Their engines roar <u>constantly</u> for all to hear.

29. The mayor gets <u>very</u> angry complaints from neighbors.

30. However, some residents <u>really</u> look forward to each plane's take-off and landing.

31. They are <u>quite</u> entertained by the power of the jets.

32. These people <u>never</u> get tired of sitting on the grassy hill and waiting for a plane to fly over.

33. The breeze blew slowly and gently.

34. The dentist worked carefully and precisely.

35. Mariah dresses colorfully.

36. The nurse spoke quietly and respectfully.

GED Skill Strategy, *pages 50–51*

Page 50

Exercise 1

1. The shipments (needs) to go out by noon today.

2. The shipping clerks brought (they) supplies to the floor.

3. He (be) the fastest worker out there now.

4. Some of the (worker's) think the pay is too low.

5. They don't move as (quick) as other workers.

6. Mrs. Vargas gives the (employees's) annual review.

7. All the clerks get (his) paycheck on Friday.

8. The accountant (take) tax deductions from their checks.

9. Mrs. Vargas (done called) the accountant today.

10. People (respects) Mrs. Vargas.

Exercise 2

There are many possible answers, depending on which mistakes you make most often.

Page 51

Exercise 3

1. yes   2. yes

Exercise 4

1. Edward, my business partner, love^s to cook.

2. ~~Him~~ He brings me a delicious lunch every Friday.

3. He has ~~did~~ done this ever since we teamed up together.

4. I pay five dollars for each one of ~~Edwards's~~ Edward's lunches.

5. I (treat) sometimes him to lunch at the corner diner.

6. ~~These~~ This is just one reason why we like being business partners.

GED Test-Taking Strategy

Page 53

1. **(1) change <u>was</u> to <u>will be</u>** The future tense is correct since the sentence contains the word *tomorrow*.

2. **(1) change <u>veteran's</u> to <u>veterans</u>** The plural noun *veterans* does not need an apostrophe.

3. **(4) no correction is necessary** The sentence is correct as written.

4. **(1) change <u>Those</u> to <u>That</u>** The correct adjective is *that* since *wound* is singular.

5. **(3) change <u>miami</u> to <u>Miami</u>** Since *Miami* is a proper noun, it should begin with a capital letter.

Unit 1 GED Test Practice, *pages 54–56*

Page 54

1. **(4) no correction is necessary** The sentence is correct as written.

2. **(2) change childs to children** The plural of *child* is *children*.

3. **(4) change sees to see** The plural *them* agrees with the verb *see*.

4. **(1) change This to These** The noun *children* is plural, so use the adjective *these*.

Page 55

5. **(3) change became to become** The correct past participle is *become*.

6. **(2) change theater's to theaters'** This is the correct way to form the possessive of the plural noun *theaters*.

7. **(3) change was to are** The correct form of the helping verb *be* is present tense, plural *are*.

8. **(1) change might to people might** To make the sentence complete, add the subject *people*.

Page 56

9. **(3) change loud to loudly** The adverb *loudly* correctly describes *talking*.

10. **(3) change its to their** The correct pronoun is *their* since the antecedent *people* is plural.

Unit 2 Lesson 10

Page 58

There are many possible ways to correct the fragments. Here are some examples.

1. <u>Paloma</u> is going to the movies.

2. <u>The wedding</u> will happen next year.

3. The large brown dog <u>barks at visitors</u>.

4. The dog's owners <u>try to quiet the dog</u>.

Page 59

1. (Maria) writes to her parents every week.

2. (Her parents) wait for those letters.

3. (Her letters) are important to them.

4. (She) writes about her job most of the time.

5. (She) tells them about her friends sometimes.

6. (They) miss her.

7. writes	9. are	11. tells
8. wait	10. writes	12. miss

There are many possible ways to rewrite the sentences. Here are some examples.

13. Marta works very hard.

14. The high school student hopes to go to college.

15. I studied all weekend.

16. A flock of pigeons landed on the statue in the park.

Lesson 11

Page 60

There are many possible ways to correct the run-on sentences. Here are some examples.

1. Tigers are cats. They have stripes.

2. The dress came in three colors; I liked the blue one best.

3. I go to work. Then I come home.

Page 62

There are many possible ways to correct the fragments. Here are some examples.

1. The mayor was answering questions at the press conference.
2. My dog is following me everywhere.
3. After I had supper, I watched TV.
4. I am hoping for rain tomorrow.
5. The dog barked at me when I got home.

Page 63

There are many possible ways to answer questions 1–8. Here are some examples.

1. Her car broke down. She called the garage.
2. There are nine planets in the solar system. The one closest to the sun is Mercury.
3. He interrupted before I could say a word.
4. My friend Vivian loves pizza.
5. They went home.
6. I left the window open.
7. Ralph is building shelves.
8. I was talking on the telephone.

Lesson 12

Page 65

1. plan
2. are
3. want
4. needs
5. are
6. expects
7. His wife, not his children, is from California.
8. The manager, as well as all of her employees, attends the meetings.
9. is
10. walks
11. hopes
12. wants

Page 66

1. Here is the letter.
2. There are three pages.
3. In front of it is an envelope.
4. At the back are order forms.
5. Where is their earlier order?
6. Here it is.
7. At the top is the date.
8. There is no signature.
9. In our garden grow all kinds of vegetables.
10. Across the street live two young couples.
11. Around the corner stands a statue of Booker T. Washington.
12. Here is your change.
13. There go the mail carriers.
14. On the next block is a shopping center.
15. There are many stores.
16. In each of them works at least one person.

Page 67

1. are
2. are
3. live
4. needs
5. meets
6. work
7. was
8. look
9. comes
10. have
11. is
12. meet
13. is
14. are
15. is
16. likes
17. enjoy
18. prefers

Lesson 13

Page 68

1. The rap singer has <u>wealth</u>, <u>talent</u>, and <u>is famous</u>. NP

2. Fame can be <u>exciting</u>, <u>rewarding</u>, and <u>it can be a challenge</u>. NP

3. We <u>dined</u>, <u>danced</u>, and <u>stayed out</u> until midnight. P

Page 69

1. Most companies today want employees with different <u>backgrounds</u>, <u>ideas</u>, and <u>skills</u>. P

2. <u>Executives</u>, <u>managers</u>, and <u>hourly workers</u> all need to get along with people different from themselves. P

3. Diversity in the workplace is <u>important</u>, <u>useful</u>, and <u>being exciting</u>. NP

4. My <u>cousin</u>, my <u>father</u>, and my <u>sister</u> all work for Union Industries. P

5. Union Industries is a <u>growing</u>, <u>smart</u>, and <u>differently</u> company. NP

6. This company holds workshops <u>regularly</u>, <u>eagerly</u>, and <u>convenient</u>. NP

7. The parking policy in this neighborhood is ~~unfairly~~, annoying, and disrespectful to the residents. unfair

8. Homeowners, renters, and landlords all have complained to city officials. P

9. They complained loudly, often, and ~~angry~~. angrily

10. People from outside the city come here, park their cars, and ~~leaving~~ their trash everywhere! leave

11. City officials plan to hold a meeting, hear residents' ideas, and ~~be planning~~ a new parking policy. plan

12. They are asking residents to make their comments respectful, brief, and ~~clearly~~. clear

GED Skill Strategy, *pages 70–71*

Page 70

Exercise 1: Ed and I are thinking about moving to Des Moines. <u>Offered a job there</u>. <u>At a radio station</u>. <u>A good opportunity</u>. The job offers a higher salary. <u>Probably will take it</u>. One of the things we want to check before we move is the school system. <u>Want the kids to have a good school</u>. Ed hopes the high school has a good football team. <u>Our son Paul starting at quarterback</u>.

There are several ways to rewrite the sentence fragments. Here are some examples.

1. I have been offered a job there.

2. The job is at a radio station.

3. It is a good opportunity.

4. We probably will take it.

5. We want the kids to have a good school.

6. Ed would love to see our son Paul starting at quarterback.

Page 71

Exercise 2: <u>Went to the company's Human Resources Department yesterday</u>. <u>Because I just got married</u>. <u>Want to extend my medical coverage to my wife</u>. I have to fill out some forms then I have to wait thirty days for insurance to take effect. <u>Not too expensive</u>. It is a good deal I am happy.

Exercise 3: There are many possible ways to rewrite the paragraph. Here is an example.

I went to the company's Human Resources Department yesterday because I just got married. I want to extend my medical insurance to my wife. I have to fill out some forms, and then I have to wait thirty days for insurance to take effect. It is not too expensive. It is a good deal. I am happy.

GED Test-Taking Strategy

Page 73

1. **(3) feel sad, lonely, and depressed** The correct series contains three adjectives: *sad, lonely, and depressed*. Now the sentence has parallel structure. Choices (1), (2), and (4) do not solve the problem with parallel structure.

2. **(2) healthy. They often smoke** The original sentence is a run-on. Choice (2) makes two complete sentences. Choices (1), (3), and (4) do not fix the run-on.

3. **(4) do not exercise often.** The correct subject-verb agreement is *They do*. The verb *do* agrees with the plural subject *They*.

4. **(3) days than men** The original version contains a sentence fragment: *Than men report*. Choice (3) correctly joins the fragment to the sentence before it. Choice (4) incorrectly joins the fragment to the sentence with a comma.

5. **(1) help keep your** The sentence is correct as written.

Unit 2 GED Test Practice, *pages 74–76*

Page 74

1. **(3) rights when they** This answer choice corrects the sentence fragment *When they cast their ballots* by joining it with the sentence before it.

2. **(4) Voters have the right** The original sentence is missing a subject. Choice (4) is the only choice that completes the fragment by adding a subject.

3. **(2) friend is allowed to help** The verb should agree with the part of the subject closest to it: *friend is allowed*.

Page 75

4. **(4) energetic** The original sentence did not have parallel structure. The correct sentence contains a series of three adjectives. Choices (1), (2), and (3) do not solve the problem in parallel structure.

5. **(2) children. They also work** Choice (2) corrects the run-on sentence by creating two separate sentences. Choices (1), (3), and (4) do not fix the run-on.

6. **(1) classroom has all kinds** The sentence is correct as written.

7. **(4) there are** The verb should agree with the subject *tips*, a plural noun. Remember that *there* is not a subject.

Page 76

8. **(4) here so that all employees** Choice (4) corrects the sentence fragment by creating one sentence. Choices (1), (2), and (3) do not correct the sentence fragment.

9. (3) closing The original sentence did not have parallel structure. The correct sentence contains a series of three *-ing* verb forms. Choices (1), (2), and (4) do not correct the problem with parallel structure.

Unit 3 Lesson 14

Page 78

Ⓟa t,

Ⓘ will help you choose a birthday present for Ⓜaria. lⒺt's meet at Ⓕranklin's Ⓥideo Ⓢtore tomorrow. Ⓘ'm sure we can find a movie your sister will like.

Ⓛeslie

Pat,

I will help you choose a birthday present for Maria. Let's meet at Franklin's Video Store tomorrow. I'm sure we can find a movie your sister will like.

Leslie

Page 79

Dear Ms. Rivera,

Lucy was Ⓗome sick for a Ⓦeek with the Ⓜeasles. Her Ⓕriend Roger brought over the Ⓗomework Ⓐssignments and told her what happened in Ⓢchool. I think Lucy is Ⓤp Ⓣo Ⓓate in her Ⓢchoolwork.

Mina Jones

Dear Ms. Rivera,

Lucy was home sick for a week with the measles. Her friend Roger brought over the homework assignments and told her what happened in school. I think Lucy is up to date in her schoolwork.

Mina Jones

Page 80

1. My son's favorite book is *Green Eggs and Ham*.
2. He also loves *Where the Wild Things Are*.
3. *I Love Lucy* is an old TV show that is still popular.
4. My family loves the movie *Butch Cassidy and the Sundance Kid*.

Page 81

1. I did my best, and I got the job.
2. I thought the *Lord of the Rings* movies were good.
3. Tim took his son Adam to the clinic.
4. Wilma told me you fixed the leaky faucet.
5. We watch *The Young and the Restless* every afternoon.
6. We are going to a party tomorrow night.
7. She asked me if I'd bring my famous pasta salad.

Lesson 15

Page 82

There are many ways to answer questions 1–3. Here are some examples.

1. Today is December 6.
2. Today is Tuesday.
3. Thanksgiving is the nearest holiday.

Page 83

1. Her birthday is February 14, which is also Valentine's Day.

2. Christmas Eve is always on December 24, the day before Christmas.

3. July is usually the hottest month of the summer.

4. The weekend starts tomorrow, Saturday.

5. Last year Columbus Day was on Monday, October 18.

6. My vacation begins on Saturday, June 11, 2005.

7. Last year Thanksgiving came on Thursday, November 26.

Lesson 16

Page 84

There are many ways to answer the question. Here is an example.

Bob Riviera
Roosevelt Hospital Clinic

Page 85

There are many possible sentences. Here is an example.

I have lived at 336 West Washington St., Apartment 1 for two years.

Watertown, MA
Watertown, Massachusetts

Page 86

There are many ways to answer the questions. Here are some examples.

Julio Valez
12 14th Ave. Apt. 6C
New York, NY 10089

Lee Chan
632 Market Street
San Francisco, CA 94123

I recently visited the Vietnam Veterans Memorial in Washington, D.C.

I recently visited a monument to veterans in the nation's capital.

Page 87

1. I took my mother to see a doctor in Baltimore, Maryland.

2. My sister, Dr. Roberta P. Wong, works at the hospital.

3. Mr. Martinez showed Miss Foster how to fill out her time card.

4. Roger's minister is Rev. Calvin Franklin.

5. Please send the bill to Ms. Marilyn Stuart, 6701 Lincoln Street, Portland, ME.

6. Tourists love to visit the White House and the Washington Monument in Washington, D.C.

7. On their vacation, Mr. and Mrs. Mitzner saw the Grand Canyon, Yellowstone National Park, and two state parks.

GED Skill Strategy, *pages 88–89*

Page 88

Exercise 1: (i've) decided (i) should return to (texas) to be closer to my parents. (my) wife (barbara) agrees. (we) will be happier there than we have been in (kansas) . (we) will probably live in (dallas) or perhaps in (houston).

Exercise 2: I come from Ho Chi Minh City in the south of Vietnam. It used to be called Saigon. Now I live in Canada. I moved with my family to Toronto. It is the capital of the province of Ontario. It is a nice city, and I like it very much.

Page 89

Exercise 3: The Salton Sea is a shallow (Salt) (Lake) about 370 square miles in area. It is located in California. It was formed by the flooding of the Colorado River. The (River) flooded around the (Year) 1905.

Exercise 4: In 1891 the famous scientist Marie Curie went to Paris, France, to study chemistry and physics. She came from Poland. She and her husband, Pierre, discovered the element radium. Marie Curie was the first person to be awarded the Nobel Prize twice.

Lesson 17

Page 90

There are many ways to answer the questions. Here are some examples.

1. I like Korean food.
2. Do you think you can meet me after work for dinner?
3. I just got a new job!

Page 91

1. I ran an ad in the newspaper.
2. It looked like it would be easy to get a job.
3. At work I type, file, and answer the phone.
4. This is really an amazing surprise!
5. Did my husband help you plan the party?
6. This is an emergency!

7. Is she all right?
8. You were asleep when your mother called.
9. How many planets are in the solar system?
10. Is the moon a planet?
11. Moons are not considered planets.
12. Some planets have more than one moon.
13. Jupiter has several moons.
14. What is a hacksaw?
15. A hacksaw cuts through metal.
16. Do you know the differences among a hacksaw, a crosscut saw, and a ripsaw?

Lesson 18

Page 93

The seven continents are Asia, Africa, North America, South America, Europe, Australia, and Antarctica.

Page 94

1. NC
2. NC
3. C Myra received a good review, and she was promised a raise.

Page 95

1. The Declaration of Independence discusses life, liberty, and the pursuit of happiness.
2. Michael Phelps, who is an American swimmer, won eight medals in the 2004 Olympics.
3. I saw lions, tigers, and bears at the zoo.
4. Yes, the Sears Tower is in Chicago.
5. Fluffy, my kitten, is Siamese.
6. I met Jason Kidd, the famous basketball player.
7. Would you prefer coffee, tea, or milk?
8. Aaron, I need you to clean your room.
9. We went shopping yesterday, but we didn't buy anything.
10. Natalie, who is rarely sick, has a doctor's appointment.
11. Tanya, who is my eldest niece, is getting married.
12. She asked me to be her matron of honor, and I agreed.
13. Tanya's mother, my sister Janice, will plan the wedding.
14. She will send the invitations and prepare the food.
15. The guests will include the couple's families, friends, and co-workers.
16. Tanya's fiancé, Terrence, is a cable installer.
17. They will live in Terrence's apartment, but they hope to own a home someday.
18. I wish them health, happiness, and a long life together.

Lesson 19

Page 96

It's time that the people of this state look closely at each candidate. I'm the only one who'd be a good governor. If elected, I'll lower taxes and reduce unemployment. I'll encourage industry to build factories here. My opponent can't promise this. You're the voters; you'll make the difference in this election.

Page 97

1. team's
2. arena's
3. night's
4. coach's
5. ours
6. crowd's
7. theirs
8. yours
9. rookie's

Page 99

1. "Let's go to the Brooklyn Museum," said Maria.
2. "Is that near the aquarium?" Bruce asked.
3. "No, it is next to the Botanical Garden," Maria explained.
4. "Oh!" Bruce replied. "I know where that is."
5. "You could all come to my house afterwards," suggested my friend.
6. "Say, that's a great idea!" exclaimed Tina.
7. An explorer's life is full of adventures and surprises.
8. Vasco da Gama's ships sailed to India.
9. Jacques Cartier explored Canada's coast.
10. Ponce de Leon's adventures included searching for a fountain of youth.
11. Ferdinand Magellan crossed the world's oceans.

12. Marco Polo explored Asia's great land.

13. It's

14. didn't

15. wasn't

16. I'll

17. don't

Lesson 20

Page 101

1. Who's

2. you're

3. your

4. It's

5. their

6. You're

7. We're

8. Were

9. Whose

10. It's, its

11. They're, their

12. It's, your

13. Their, its

14. you're, you're

Page 102

1. see, sea

2. know, way

3. writes

4. Our, hour

5. read

6. to, too

Page 103

1. We're

2. You're

3. it's

4. They're

5. there

6. Who's

7. Whose

8. your

9. Their

10. no

11. be

12. pain

13. red

14. whole

15. two

16. see

17. rights

18. peace

19. weight

20. to

Lesson 21

Page 104

1. (freind)   friend

2. (reciept)   receipt

3. (hieght)   height

Page 105

1. worked   working

2. lived   living

3. planned   planning

4. talked   talking

5. reminded   reminding

Page 106

1. leisure

2. ancient

3. science

4. foreign

5. Neither

6. receive

7. louder   loudest

8. thinner   thinnest

9. kinder   kindest

10. madder   maddest

11. finer   finest

12. softer   softest

13. stopped   stopping

14. loved   loving

15. controlled   controlling

16. referred   referring

17. stressed   stressing

18. ruled   ruling

19. shopped   shopping

20. fixed   fixing

Page 107

21. preferred	**25.** remembering
22. niece	**26.** younger
23. height	**27.** permitted
24. skating	**28.** relief

If you are (haveing) computer trouble, CompWiz can help. We are experts in repairing any problem for any computer we (recieve) in our shop. Does your computer seem slow and (slugish)? Let us help you get rid of (unneedded) files. We are (commited) to our customers, and we guarantee satisfaction. You come as a customer, and you leave as a (freind).

If you are having computer trouble, CompWiz can help. We are experts in repairing any problem for any computer we receive in our shop. Does your computer seem slow and sluggish? Let us help you get rid of unneeded files. We are committed to our customers, and we guarantee satisfaction. You come as a customer, and you leave as a friend.

GED Skill Strategy, pages 108–109

Page 108

Exercise 1: Good morning, dieters! Are you tired of eating the same old breakfast?
Do you want a change?
Are you worried about fat and calories?
Then try our new low-calorie, high-fiber carrot muffin.

Exercise 2: It's a delicious new breakfast treat. It has no sugar, fat, or preservatives. It's packed with fiber and real carrots. You'll love it!
There are many possible ways to end the ad. Here is an example.
Try it for breakfast tomorrow!

Page 109

Exercise 3: The pyramids, which are huge stone structures, were built 5,000 years ago in Egypt. Scientists still wonder how they were built.

Exercise 4: Who built the pyramids? Thousands of Egyptian slaves, who were forced to work for the pharaoh, labored for hundreds of years. They had no modern tools. How did they lift those gigantic blocks? Scientists think that they used levers, pulleys, and block-and-tackle. We may never know for sure, and we will always try to discover more.

GED Test-Taking Strategy

Page 111

1. **(4) change soldier's to soldiers** There is no need for an apostrophe in the plural noun *soldiers*.

2. **(3) change hour to our** *Hour* means "60 minutes"; *our* means "belonging to us."

3. **(2) change united states to United States** The name of a specific country is always capitalized.

4. **(4) change Libraries to libraries** The noun *libraries* is a general term. It does not name a specific person, place, or thing.

Unit 3 GED Test Practice, pages 112–114

Page 112

1. **(2) change Weeks to weeks** The noun *weeks* does not need to be capitalized.

2. **(3) change write to right** The two words sound the same, but *right* is the correct word to use in this sentence.

3. **(2) insert a comma after <u>boxes</u>** A comma is needed after each item in the series: *boxes*, *tape*, and *newspaper*.

4. **(4) change <u>freinds</u> to <u>friends</u>** *Friends* follows the "i before e" rule.

Page 113

5. **(3) insert a comma after <u>attendant</u>** A comma is used to separate the name *Angela Delgado* from the title *attendant*.

6. **(1) change <u>delgado</u> to <u>Delgado</u>** *Delgado* is a person's last name and should be capitalized.

7. **(2) change the question mark to a period** The sentence is a statement and should end with a period.

8. **(3) change <u>june</u> to <u>June</u>** *June* is a specific month and should be capitalized.

Page 114

9. **(3) change <u>its</u> to <u>it's</u>** *It's* is the contraction for the words *it is*.

Unit 4 Lesson 22

Page 116

There are many ways to write the thank-you note. Here is an example.

Dear Jackie,

Thank you for the clothes and toys that Billy has outgrown. The clothes are just the right size for Randy. He looks especially handsome in the blue shirt with the cars on it. And he loves playing with all his new bath toys.

Laura

Page 117

There are many ways to write the note with directions. Share your work with your teacher.

Lesson 23

Page 119

1. P
2. P
3. NP
4. NP

There are many possible sentences that support each topic sentence. Here are some examples.

5. Having money can take away some of your worries. However, it cannot buy you true friends.

6. It stormed all day Saturday and Sunday. The wind knocked out the electricity in our neighborhood.

Lesson 24

Page 121

There are many ways to write your topic, purpose, and notes. Share your work with your teacher.

1. <u>My new years resilution was to become more activ.</u>

2. There are many possible paragraphs. Share your work with your teacher.

Page 122

Share your edited paragraph with your teacher.

Page 123

There are many possible paragraphs. Share your work with your teacher.

Lesson 25

Page 125

There are many possible narrative paragraphs. Here is an example of a final version.

My neighbor, Olivia Ponce, did an extremely brave thing last week. Olivia donated a kidney to her younger sister, who has advanced kidney disease. The operation was at 7 a.m. on Wednesday morning. Doctors at Hayes Memorial performed the operations on Olivia and her sister. The operations were a success. I wish Olivia and her sister all the best.

Lesson 26

Page 126

I grew up in a small town in Kansas. It was mostly farmland, with green fields extending in all directions. Our neighbors grew tall yellow corn, large red tomatoes, and juicy green lettuce. Some farmers raised brown, black, and white cows. In the evenings we could hear the cows mooing. At night the air was cool and crisp. There were millions of bright stars in the dark black sky.

There are many ways to complete the exercise. Here is an example.

My dog Ranger is a mutt. I got him when he was a tiny _{young} puppy. He has long _{curly} brown _{dark} hair, soft floppy ears, and a little _{short} tail that he wags all the time. He runs fast to chase a stick and jumps high to catch a ball. His loud _{high} bark warns me that someone is at the door. Ranger is my best _{trusted} friend.

Page 127

There are many possible descriptive paragraphs. Share your work with your teacher.

Lesson 27

Page 128

To do a push-up, first lie face down on the floor. Second, flex your feet so your toes are on the floor and your heels are sticking up. Next, put your palms on the floor beside your shoulders. Then, straighten your arms and push yourself up, keeping your back straight. Finally, bend your arms and lower your body. Don't collapse! Repeat.

Page 129

There are many possible explanatory paragraphs. Here is an example of a final version.

To make Sarita's Special Scrambled Eggs, first break two large eggs into a bowl. Next add 1 tablespoon of chopped onion. Then add some crumbled Monterey Jack cheese. Use as much as you like. Last, add $\frac{1}{2}$ teaspoon of red pepper flakes. Mix with a fork. Finally, pour the eggs into a buttered frying pan, and stir with a fork until eggs are cooked.

Lesson 28

Page 130

There are many possible ways to answer questions 1–3. Here are some examples.

1. Horacio Gomez should be re-elected.
2. Crime in the city went down.
   The city has a new hospital.
3. Vote for Horacio Gomez for mayor.

Page 131

There are many possible persuasive paragraphs. Here is an example of a final version.

I think that baseball players earn too much money. They work hard, and they practice, but they don't work twelve months of the year the way the rest of us do. Also, being a good ballplayer is a skill you are born with. These guys don't go to school for many years like doctors. All these million-dollar salaries just raise the price of tickets to the ballpark, so I can't afford to take my kids to games.

GED Skill Strategy, *pages 132–133*

Page 132

Exercise 1

There are many possible answers. Here are some examples.

2. main point: Applying for a job is hard work.
   details: read the want ads, fill out application, going to interview
   topic sentence: Applying for a job is hard work because there are several steps involved.

3. main point: Carlotta
   details: friends for 10 years, very supportive, like a sister to me
   topic sentence: My best friend, Carlotta, has been there for me every day for 10 years.

Page 133

Exercise 2

1. ~~I once took a vacation in the fall~~.
2. ~~My cousin wants to be a plumber~~.

Exercise 3

There are many possible topic sentences. Here are some examples.

1. Mary is a terrific employee.
2. To succeed as a childcare worker, a person must have special qualities.

GED Test-Taking Strategy

Page 135

There are many ways to respond to the topics. Share your work with your teacher.

Unit 4 GED Test Practice, *pages 136–138*

Pages 136–138

There are many ways to respond to the topics. Share your work with your teacher.

Writing Posttest, *pages 140–145*

Page 140

1. **(2) change were to was** The verb *was* agrees with the singular subject *it*.

2. **(4) change you're to your** The possessive pronoun *your* is correct; it is not a contraction and does not need an apostrophe.

3. **(3) change sudden to suddenly** The adverb *suddenly* describes the verb *were gone*.

4. **(1) change weve to we've** *We've* is a contraction of *we have*, so an apostrophe is needed.

Page 141

5. **(4) no correction is necessary** The sentence is correct as written.

6. **(3) change grocerys to groceries** The correct plural form is *groceries*.

7. **(2) change they're to their** The possessive pronoun *their* is correct.

8. **(1) change taked to take** The correct form of the verb is *take*.

Page 142

9. **(3) handbook and signing** This choice corrects the sentence fragment.

10. **(1) assistants are available** The underlined portion of the sentence is correct as written.

11. **(4) effective, and productive** This choice makes the sentence parallel.

12. **(2) Monday. It is an important** This choice gets rid of the run-on sentence.

Page 143

13. **(4) change Garden to garden** The noun *garden* should not be capitalized.

14. **(3) change may to May** The noun *May* names a specific month and should be capitalized.

15. **(2) insert a comma after grow** A comma is needed to join the two complete thoughts with *and*.

16. **(4) no correction is necessary** The sentence is correct as written.

Page 144

17. **(2) remove the comma after night** A comma is not needed in this sentence.

18. **(2) change Mother to mother** The noun *mother* should not be capitalized.

19. **(2) change did'nt to didn't** The apostrophe should replace the letter or letters left out in the contraction: *did not = didn't*.

20. **(1) change recieved to received** The spelling rule is that *e* should come before *i* when preceded by a *c*.

Page 145

21. Paragraphs will vary. Share your paragraph with your teacher.